Jewelry Designs with CzechMates Beads

Anna Elizabeth Draeger

Kalmbach Books
21027 Crossroads Circle
Waukesha, Wisconsin 53186
www.JewelryAndBeadingStore.com

Published in 2017
21 20 19 18 17   1 2 3 4 5

Manufactured in China

ISBN: 978-1-62700-318-6
EISBN: 978-1-62700-319-3

Editor: Erica Swanson
Book Design: Lisa Schroeder
Technical Editor: Dana Meredith
Illustrator: Kellie Jaeger
Photographer: William Zuback

Library of Congress Control Number: 2016943700

Jewelry Designs with CzechMates Beads

Anna Elizabeth Draeger

KALMBACH BOOKS

Waukesha, Wisconsin

Contents

Introduction

As a jewelry designer, I see how beads fit into shapes that I observe in the world around me. With new bead styles being released at the speed of light these days, it amazes me that I can apply that inspiration when creating my jewelry designs. This collection showcases CzechMates beads, two- and four-hole beads that are designed to be interchanged, substituted, and combined for endless possibilities.

I used CzechMates beads throughout this book to create components that can be used in various ways. You can make an everyday bracelet, a stunning necklace, or even a pair of earrings to match. The CzechMates beads used in this book are Bar, Triangle, Lentil, Crescent, Dagger, Brick, Tile, QuadraTile, and QuadraLentil beads. Other beads used are my normal fare: 3–4mm bicone crystals and pearls, 2–3mm rondelle crystals, seed beads, and a few other accent beads, such as DiamonDuos.

Like my other books, this volume uses modification of some of my favorite stitches, including peyote, herringbone, right-angle weave, and other basic beadweaving techniques. I used Tulip #12 needles and 6- or 8-lb. test Fireline for most projects because of the strength. I've been experimenting with other fishing lines that have the same attributes, like nanofil, which is thinner but just as strong.

It is my goal for people to create beautiful, handmade things. So many people are afraid to begin a project because it looks too intricate, but my illustrations will take you through each project, step by step. The awesomeness about beading is that although a pattern might result in a bracelet, you can apply the skills you learn when creating your own designs.

I'm really excited to share these designs with you, and hope you get a lot of enjoyment from them. As always, I'm available for any questions you run into with the designs—but just remember, sometimes certain shapes and colors leave the bead world, so use your own color sense to pick the colors you love.

Happy beading!

— Anna

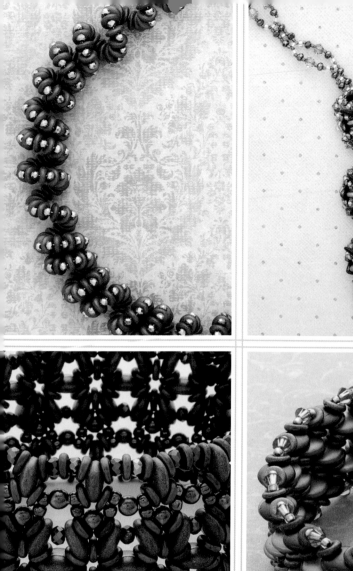

Basics

You'll only need a handful of tools, the right beads, and a few easy
stitching techniques to create gorgeous jewelry.

CZECHMATES BEADS

CzechMates are designed to work interchangeably within a jewelry project. For many pieces, you can substitute one two- or four-hole bead for another. You can also combine shapes, as the holes are all spaced equally. CzechMates are available in many different colors and finishes. You can find many options at your local bead or craft stores.

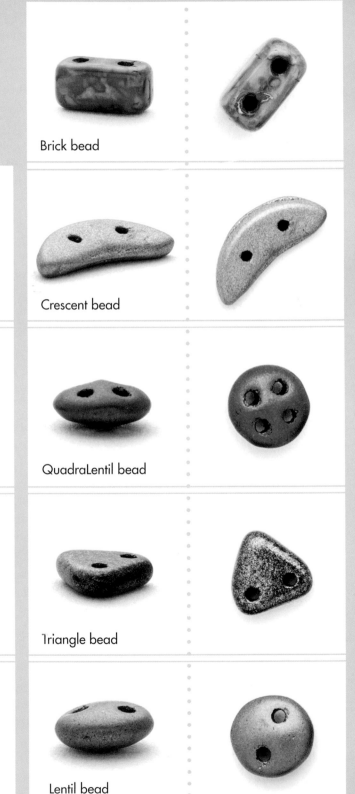

Brick bead

QuadraTile bead

Crescent bead

Bar bead

QuadraLentil bead

Tile bead

Triangle bead

Dagger bead

Lentil bead

9

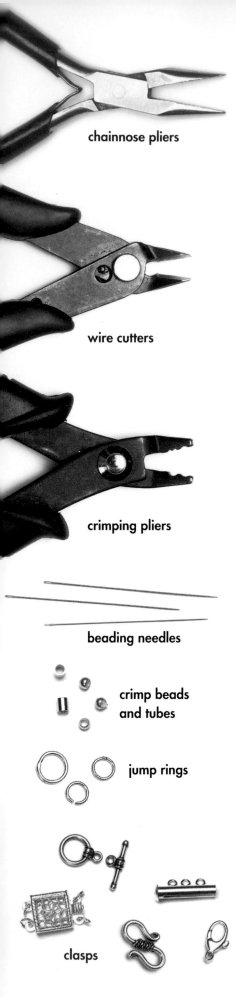

chainnose pliers

wire cutters

crimping pliers

beading needles

crimp beads
and tubes

jump rings

clasps

TOOLS & MATERIALS

Excellent tools and materials for making jewelry are available in bead and craft stores, through catalogs, and online. Here are the essential supplies you'll need for the projects in this book.

Tools

Chainnose pliers have smooth, flat inner jaws, and the tips taper to a point. Use them for gripping, bending wire, and for opening and closing loops and jump rings.

Use the front of a **wire cutters'** blades to make a pointed cut and the back of the blades to make a flat cut.

Crimping pliers have two grooves in their jaws that are used to fold and roll a crimp bead into a compact shape.

Beading needles are coded by size. The higher the number, the finer the beading needle. Unlike sewing needles, the eye of a beading needle is almost as narrow as its shaft. In addition to the size of the bead, the number of times you will pass through the bead also affects the needle size that you will use; if you will pass through a bead multiple times, you need to use a thinner needle.

Findings

A **jump ring** is used to connect components. It is a small wire circle or oval that is either soldered closed or comes with a cut so it can be opened and closed.

Crimp beads and tubes are small, large-holed, thin-walled metal beads designed to be flattened or crimped into a tight roll. Use them when stringing jewelry on flexible beading wire to attach clasps.

Clasps come in many sizes and shapes. Some of the most common are the toggle, consisting of a ring and a bar; slide, consisting of one tube that slides inside another; lobster claw, which opens when you pull on a tiny lever; S-hook, which links two soldered jump rings or split rings; and box, with a tab and a slot.

Earring findings come in a huge variety of metals and styles, including (from left to right) hoop, post, French hook, and lever back. You will almost always want a loop (or loops) on earring findings so you can attach beads.

earring findings

Stitching and Stringing Materials

Selecting beading thread and cord is one of the most important decisions you'll make when planning a project. Review the descriptions below to evaluate which material is best for your design.

Parallel filament nylon, such as Nymo or C-Lon, is made from many thin nylon fibers that are extruded and heat-set to form a single-ply thread. Parallel filament nylon is durable and easy to thread, but it can be prone to fraying and stretching. It is best used in beadweaving and bead embroidery.

Plied nylon thread, such as Silamide, is made from two or more nylon threads that are extruded, twisted together, and coated or bonded for further strength, making them strong and durable. It is more resistant to fraying than parallel filament nylon, and some brands do not stretch. It's a good material for twisted fringe, bead crochet, and beadwork that needs a lot of body.

Parallel filament GSP, such as Fireline, is a single-ply thread made from spun and bonded polyethylene fibers. It's extremely strong, it doesn't stretch, and it resists fraying. However, crystals will cut through parallel filament GSP, and smoke-colored varieties can leave a black residue on hands and beads. It's most appropriate for bead stitching.

Flexible beading wire is composed of wires twisted together and covered with nylon. This wire is stronger than thread and does not stretch. The higher the number of inner strands (between 3 and 49), the more flexible and kink-resistant the wire. It is available in a variety of sizes.

flexible beading wire

parallel filament GSP

nylon threads

seed beads

Czech seed beads

Seed Beads

A huge variety of beads is available, but the beads most commonly used in the projects in this book are seed beads. Seed beads come in packages, tubes, and hanks. A standard hank (a looped bundle of beads strung on thread) contains 12 20-in. (51cm) strands, but vintage hanks are often much smaller. Tubes and packages are usually measured in grams and vary in size.

Seed beads have been manufactured in many sizes ranging from the largest, 2º, 5º, (also called "E beads"), which are about 5mm wide, to tiny size 20º or 22º, which aren't much larger than grains of sand. (The symbol º stands for "aught" or "zero." The greater the number of aughts, e.g., 22º, the smaller the bead.) Beads smaller than Japanese 15ºs have not been produced for the past 100 years, but vintage beads can be found in limited sizes and colors. The most commonly available size in the widest range of colors is 11º.

Most round seed beads are made in Japan and the Czech Republic. Czech seed beads are slightly irregular and rounder than Japanese seed beads, which are uniform in size and a bit squared off. Czech beads give a bumpier surface when woven, but they reflect light at a wider range of angles. Japanese seed beads produce a uniform surface and texture. Japanese and Czech seed beads can be used together, but a Japanese seed bead is slightly larger than the same size Czech seed bead.

Crystals

Of all the crystal shapes available, the bicone is definitely my number-one choice. As in my first book, most of the designs in this book feature bicone crystals. Bicones are versatile, economical, and quintessential crystal beads. The Xilion, the patented bicone crystal shape from the Swarovski Elements line, is even more sparkly than the traditional bicone crystal, and can be used whenever bicones are called for.

I also love to work with Swarovski Elements crystal pearls, which are beautifully perfect imitations of natural pearls. A spherical crystal core gives crystal pearls the weight of real pearls, and they are available in many gorgeous colors. The holes are consistent and larger than those in natural pearls, so they are easy to incorporate into stitching projects. Each pearl in the strand is perfectly consistent with the next.

Fire-Polished Beads

Fire-polished beads are slightly oval, with lovely facets that catch the light to mimic the look of crystal beads. They come in a large variety of colors and finishes to add an economical component to jewelry design.

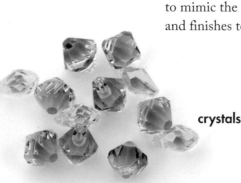

crystals

TECHNIQUES

CRIMPING

Use crimping pliers and crimp beads to secure the ends of flexible beading wire:

1 Position the crimp bead in the notch closest to the handle of the crimping pliers. Hold the wires apart to make sure one wire is on each side of the dent, and squeeze the pliers to compress the crimp bead.

2 Position the crimp bead in the notch near the tip of the pliers with the dent facing the tips. Squeeze the pliers to fold the crimp in half. Tug on the wires to make sure the crimp is secure.

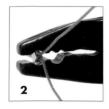

OPENING AND CLOSING PLAIN LOOPS, JUMP RINGS, AND EARRING FINDINGS

1 Hold a loop or a jump ring with two pairs of pliers.

2 To open the loop or jump ring, bring the tips of one pair of pliers toward you, and push the tips of the other pair away from you. Reverse the steps to close.

CONDITIONING THREAD

Use either beeswax or synthetic micro-crystalline wax (not candle wax or paraffin) or Thread Heaven to condition nylon thread (Nymo). Beeswax or synthetic wax smooths the nylon fibers and adds tackiness that will stiffen your beadwork slightly. Thread Heaven adds a static charge that causes the thread to repel itself, so don't use it with doubled thread. Stretch the thread, then pull it through the conditioner, starting with the end that comes off the spool first. Conditioning helps to protect the thread from fraying.

ADDING AND ENDING THREAD

To add a thread, sew into the beadwork several rows prior to the point where the last bead was added. Weave through the beadwork, following the existing thread path. Tie a few half-hitch knots between beads, and exit where the last stitch ended. To end a thread, weave back into the beadwork, following the existing thread path and tying two or three half-hitch knots between beads as you go. Change directions as you weave so the thread crosses itself. Sew through a few beads after the last knot, and trim the thread.

HALF-HITCH KNOT

Pass the needle under the thread between two beads. A loop will form as you pull the thread through. Cross back over the thread between the beads, sew through the loop, and pull gently to draw the knot into the beadwork.

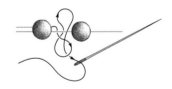

SQUARE KNOT

Bring the left-hand thread over the right-hand thread and around. Cross right over left, and go through the loop.

SURGEON'S KNOT

Bring the left-hand thread over the right-hand thread twice. Pull the ends to tighten. Cross right over left, and go through the loop. Tighten.

STOP BEAD

Use a stop bead to secure beads temporarily as you begin stitching. Choose a bead that is distinct from the beads in your project. String the stop bead, and sew through it again in the same direction. For extra security, sew through it again.

OVERHAND KNOT

Cross the ends to make a loop. Bring the end that crosses in front behind the loop, and pull it through the loop to the front. Tighten.

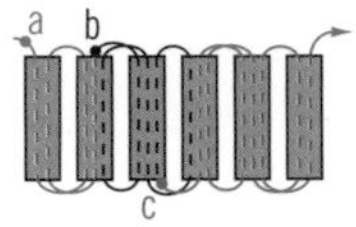

LADDER STITCH

figure 1

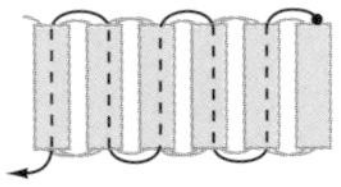

figure 2

Making a ladder

1 Pick up two beads, and sew through them both again, positioning the beads side by side so that their holes are parallel **(figure 1, a–b)**.
2 Add subsequent beads by picking up one bead, sewing through the previous bead, then sewing through the new bead **(b–c)**. Continue for the desired length.

This technique produces uneven tension, which you can correct by zigzagging back through the beads in the opposite direction **(figure 2)**, or by using the "Crossweave method."

HERRINGBONE STITCH

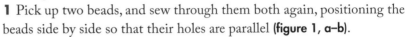
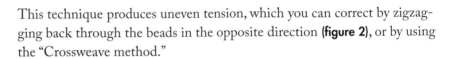

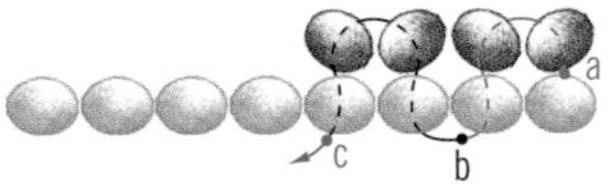

figure 1

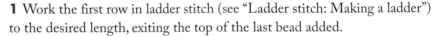

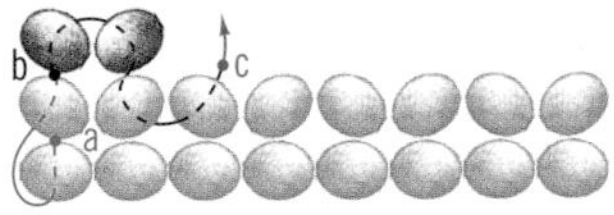

figure 2

Flat strip

1 Work the first row in ladder stitch (see "Ladder stitch: Making a ladder") to the desired length, exiting the top of the last bead added.
2 Pick up two beads, and sew down through the next bead in the previous row **(figure 1, a–b)**. Sew up through the following bead in the previous row, pick up two beads, and sew down through the next bead **(b–c)**. Repeat across the first row.
3 To turn to start the next row, sew down through the end bead in the previous row and back through the last bead of the pair just added **(figure 2, a–b)**. Pick up two beads, sew down through the next bead in the previous row, and sew up through the following bead **(b–c)**. Continue adding pairs of beads across the row.
4 To turn without having thread show on the edge, pick up an accent or smaller bead before you sew back through the last bead of the pair you just added, or work the "Concealed turn" below.

Concealed turn

To hide the thread on the edge without adding a bead for each turn, sew up through the second-to-last bead in the previous row, and continue through the last bead added **(a–b)**. Pick up two beads, sew down through the next bead in the previous row, and sew up through the following bead **(b–c)**. Continue adding pairs of beads across the row. Using this turn will flatten the angle of the edge beads, making the edge stacks look a little different than the others.

NETTING

Netting produces airy, flexible beadwork that resembles a net and can be worked vertically, horizontally, or in the round (tubular netting). Netting starts with a base row or round of beads upon which subsequent rows or rounds are stitched. Subsequent rows or rounds are added by picking up a given odd number of beads, and sewing through the center bead of the next stitch in the previous row or round.

Instructions for netting vary for each project, but some common variations include three-, five-, and seven-bead netting. The number of beads per stitch determines the drape of the overall piece. More beads per stitch produce larger spaces and a more fluid drape.

Tubular netting

1 Pick up 24 11ºs, and sew through them again to form a ring, exiting the first 11º picked up.
2 Pick up five 11ºs, skip five 11ºs in the ring, and sew through the next 11º in the ring **(a–b)**. Repeat to complete the round **(b–c)**. Step up through the first three 11ºs in the first stitch **(c–d)**.
3 Pick up five 11ºs, skip five 11ºs in the previous round, and sew through the center 11º in the next stitch in the previous round **(d–e)**. Repeat to complete the round, and step up through three 11ºs in the first stitch **(e–f)**.
4 Repeat step 3 to complete the sample.

BRICK STITCH

Work off a stitched ladder (see Ladder stitch). Pick up two beads. Sew under the thread bridge between the second and third beads on the ladder from back to front. Sew up through the second bead added and then down through the first. Come back up through the second bead. For the row's remaining stitches, pick up one bead. Sew under the next thread bridge on the previous row from back to front. Sew back up through the new bead.

ladder base

CHEVRON CHAIN

1 On a comfortable length of thread, attach a stop bead, leaving a 6-in. (15cm) tail.
2 Pick up three color-A seed beads, three color-B seed beads, three As, three color-C seed beads, three As, and three Bs **(figure 1, a–b)**. Sew back through the first three As **(b–c)**.
3 Pick up three Cs, three As, and three Bs, and sew back through the last three As added in the previous stitch **(figure 2)**.
4 Repeat step 3 **(figure 3)** to the desired length. The direction of the Vs will alternate with each stitch.

bridge
diagonal strip
connector

figure 1   **figure 2**

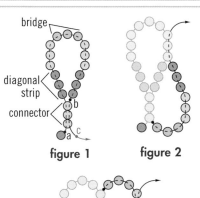

figure 3

PEYOTE STITCH

Flat even-count

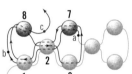

1 Pick up an even number of beads **(a–b)**. These beads will shift to form the first two rows.

2 To begin row 3, pick up a bead, skip the last bead picked up in the previous step, and sew back through the next bead **(b–c)**. For each stitch, pick up a bead, skip a bead in the previous row, and sew through the next bead, exiting the first bead picked up **(c–d)**. The beads added in this row are higher than the previous rows and are referred to as "up-beads."

3 For each stitch in subsequent rows, pick up a bead, and sew through the next up-bead in the previous row **(d–e)**. To count peyote stitch rows, count the total number of beads along both straight edges.

Flat odd-count

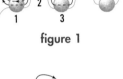

figure 1

Odd-count peyote is the same as even-count peyote, except for the turn on odd-numbered rows, where the last bead of the row can't be attached in the usual way because there is no up-bead to sew through.

Work the traditional odd-row turn as follows:

1 Begin as for flat even-count peyote, but pick up an odd number of beads. Work row 3 as in even-count, stopping before adding the last two beads.

2 Work a figure-8 turn at the end of row 3: Pick up the next-to-last bead (#7), and sew through #2, then #1 **(figure 1, a–b)**. Pick up the last bead of the row (#8), and sew through #2, #3, #7, #2, #1, and #8 **(b–c)**.

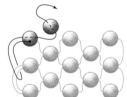

figure 2

You can work this turn at the end of each odd-numbered row, but this edge will be stiffer than the other. Instead, in subsequent odd-numbered rows, pick up the last bead of the row, then sew under the thread bridge immediately below. Sew back through the last bead added to begin the next row **(figure 2)**.

Zipping up or joining

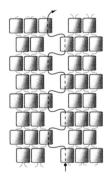

To zip up (join) two sections of a flat peyote piece invisibly, match up the two end rows and zigzag through the up-beads on both ends.

CROSSWEAVE TECHNIQUE

Crossweave is a beading technique in which you string one or more beads on both ends of a length of thread or cord and then cross the ends through one or more beads.

RIGHT-ANGLE WEAVE

figure 1

Flat strip

1 To start the first row of right-angle weave, pick up four beads, and tie them into a ring (see "Square knot"). Sew through the first three beads again **(figure 1)**.

2 Pick up three beads. Sew through the last bead in the previous stitch **(figure 2, a–b)**. Continue through the first two beads picked up **(b–c)**.

3 Continue adding three beads per stitch until the first row is the desired length **(figure 3)**.

figure 2

You are stitching in a figure-8 pattern, alternating the direction of the thread path for each stitch **(figure 3)**.

figure 3

Forming a strip into a ring

Exit the end bead of the last stitch, pick up a bead, and sew through the end bead of the first stitch. Pick up a bead, and sew through the end bead of the last stitch. Retrace the thread path to reinforce the join.

Adding rows

1 To add a row, sew through the last stitch of row 1, exiting an edge bead along one side **(figure 1)**.

2 Pick up three beads, and sew through the edge bead your thread exited in the previous step **(figure 2, a–b)**. Continue through the first new bead **(b–c)**.

3 Pick up two beads, and sew back through the next edge bead in the previous row and the bead your thread exited at the start of this step **(figure 3, a–b)**. Continue through the two new beads and the following edge bead in the previous row **(b–c)**.

4 Pick up two beads, and sew through the last two beads your thread exited in the previous stitch and the first new bead. Continue working a figure-8 thread path, picking up two beads per stitch for the rest of the row **(figure 4)**.

figure 1

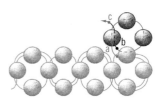

figure 2

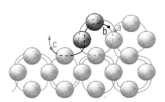

figure 3

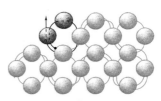

figure 4

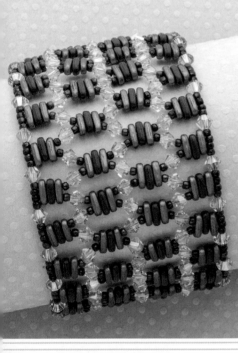

Projects

Three-Drop Pendant

COMBINE THREE CIRCULAR COMPONENTS TO STITCH UP ONE GORGEOUS NECKLACE. YOU WILL ALSO USE MULTIPLE CZECHMATES BEADS IN THIS DESIGN FOR A TRULY MULTI-HOLE STATEMENT.

Lentil bead

Crescent bead

Triangle bead

○ 11º seed bead

● 15º seed bead

⬡ 4mm crystal

 2mm rondelle

CZECHMATES
Crescent, Lentil, and Triangle beads

TECHNIQUES
- Adding and Ending Thread, p. 13
- Opening and Closing Jump Rings, p. 13

SKILL LEVEL
Intermediate ●●●

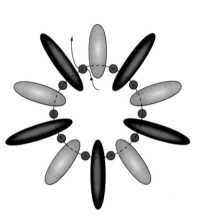

figure 1

figure 2

Tip
Lay out the Crescent beads as if they are smiling at you.

MAKE THE COMPONENTS

1. Thread a needle on 1 yd. (.9m) of Fireline, and pick up a repeating pattern of a 15º seed bead, the left hole of a Crescent bead from top down, a 15º, and a Lentil bead five times, leaving a 6-in. (15cm) tail. Sew through the same holes again, and exit a 15º after a Lentil **(figure 1)**. Your thread should be pointing to the left. Lay out the Triangle beads with the holes at the bottom.

2. Pick up two 11º seed beads and the left hole of a Triangle from top down (if your thread is exiting to the right, you will want to pick up the Triangle from the right hole first). Pick up three 11ºs, sew back through the right hole of the Triangle from bottom up, and then pick up two 11ºs. Sew through the 15º before the Lentil, the Lentil, and the 15º your thread exited at the start of this step. Continue through the beads in the initial ring to exit the 15º after the next Lentil in the ring, with the thread pointing to the left **(figure 2)**. Repeat this step four times to complete the round, and then sew through the beadwork to exit the three 11ºs at the tip of any Triangle.

SUPPLIES
- **16** Lentil beads
- **12** Crescent beads
- **12** Triangle beads
- **12** 4mm bicone crystals
- **28** 4mm bicone crystals (for strap)
- 5x10mm (or 7x13mm) crystal top-drilled pendant
- **28** 2mm crystals, round or rondelle
- **100** 2mm crystals, round or rondelle (for strap)
- **3–4g** 15º seed beads
- **4–5g** 11º seed beads
- Clasp
- **2–4** 6mm jump rings
- Fireline, 6- or 8-lb. test
- Beading needles, #12

figure 3

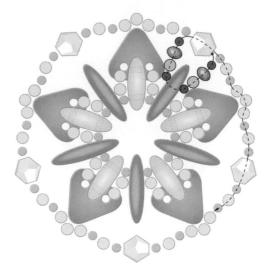

figure 4

3. Pick up a 15º, an 11º, a 15º, a 4mm, a 15º, an 11º, and a 15º. Sew through the three 11ºs at the tip of the next Triangle. Repeat this step to complete the round, retrace the thread path, and then exit a 4mm **(figure 3)**.

4. Pick up a 15º, an 11º, a 2mm, an 11º, and a 15º. Sew back through the open hole of the nearest Crescent. Pick up a 15º, an 11º, a 2mm, an 11º, and a 15º. Sew through the 4mm again, and retrace the thread path, gently snugging up the beads. Sew through the next ten beads to exit the next 4mm **(figure 4)**. Repeat this step to complete the round. Set the working thread aside; it will be used to connect the components.

5. Make two more components as the first, but for the second component, only pick up a repeating pattern four times in step 1, and for the third component, only pick up a repeating pattern three times in step 1. End all the tails.

6. Using the remaining thread from the first component, exit the center 11º at the tip of a Triangle. Pick up a 15º, a 2mm, and a 15º. Sew through the center 11º from the tip of a Triangle on the second component. Pick up a 15º, a 2mm, and a 15º. Sew through the center 11º from the tip of the Triangle on the first component. Retrace the thread path several times, and end the working thread from the first component **(figure 5)**.

7. Using the remaining thread from the second component, exit the center 11º at the tip of a Triangle opposite the join to the first component. Pick up a 15º, a 2mm, and a 15º. Sew through the center 11º from the tip of a Triangle on the third component. Pick up a 15º, a 2mm, and a 15º. Sew through the center 11º from the tip of the Triangle on the second component. Retrace the thread path several times, and end the working thread from the second component.

8. Using the remaining thread from the third component, exit a 4mm opposite the join to the second component. Pick up a 15º, an 11º, a 15º, a Lentil, a 15º, a Lentil, a 15º, a crystal pendant, a 15º, a Lentil, a 15º, a Lentil, a 15º, an 11º, and a 15º. Sew through the 4mm your thread exited at the start of this step, retrace the thread path several times, and then end the working thread from the third component.

NECKLACE STRAP
1. Center 3 yd. (2.8m) of thread at the top of the first component so the tail exits the center 11º at the tip of one Triangle, and the working thread exits the center 11º at the tip of the next Triangle **(figure 6, a–b)**.

2. With the working thread, * pick up a 15º, a 2mm, a 15º, an 11º, a 15º, a 2mm, and a 15º. Sew through the center 11º at the tip of the Triangle, and then through the first four beads picked up to exit the new 11º **(b–c)**.

3. Pick up a 15º, a 2mm, a 15º, an 11º, a 15º, a 2mm, and a 15º. Sew through the center 11º your thread exited at the start of this stitch, and then through the first four beads picked up to exit the new 11º **(c–d)**.

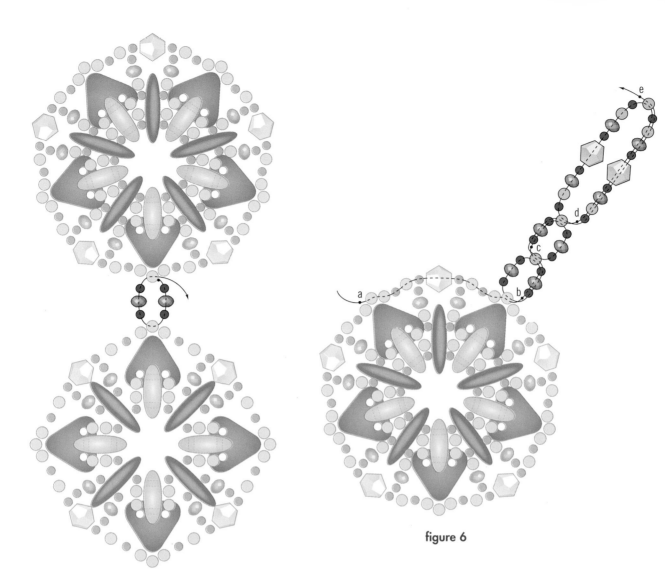

figure 5

figure 6

4. Pick up a 15º, an 11º, a 2mm, a 15º, a 4mm, a 15º, a 2mm, an 11º, a 15º, an 11º, a 15º, an 11º, a 2mm, a 15º, a 4mm, a 15º, a 2mm, an 11º, and a 15º. Sew through the center 11º your thread exited at the start of this stitch, and then sew through the next ten beads to exit the top 11º **(d–e)**.

5. Continue in this manner from * until you reach the desired length. Retrace the thread path, and end the thread (Techniques, p. 13).

6. Make a second necklace strap using the tail.

7. Attach a clasp to the end rings of the beaded necklace with jump rings (Techniques).

CLOSE-UP OF COMPONENT

Bamboo Bangle

USING A SIMPLE STRINGING TECHNIQUE, PAIR TWO-HOLE BEADS TO MAKE AN EASY-TO-WEAR BANGLE OR BRACELET. THIS DESIGN COMES TOGETHER QUICKLY, SO YOU CAN MAKE A BUNCH TO STACK ON YOUR WRIST.

Lentil bead

8º seed bead

15º seed bead

CZECHMATES
Lentil, Crescent, or Bar beads

TECHNIQUES
- Adding and Ending Thread, p. 13
- Stop Bead, p. 13
- Opening and Closing Jump Rings, p. 13 (optionall)

SKILL LEVEL
Beginner ● ○ ○

SUPPLIES
- **50–62** Lentil beads (**25–31** of each color, if using 2 colors)
- 3g 8º seed beads
- 2g 15º seed beads
- Fireline, 6- or 8-lb. test
- Beading needle, #12
- Clasp (optional)
- **2** 4mm jump rings (optional)
- **2** pairs of chainnose pliers (optional)

figure 1

MAKE THE BRACELET

1. Thread a needle and attach a stop bead to the end of 2 yd. (1.8m) of Fireline so you are working with 1 yd. (.9m) of doubled Fireline, leaving a 6-in. (15cm) tail. (If you are working with Crescent beads, lay out the beads on your work surface so they are all facing the same direction. If you are using more than one color, alternate them on your work surface as desired.)

2. Pick up an alternating pattern of a Lentil bead, an 8º seed bead, a Lentil, and a 15º seed bead **(figure 1)** until you reach the desired length. (If you are working with Crescents, pick up the same hole of the Crescents so they are all facing the same direction.)

figure 2

figure 3

Tip
- If you are making a bangle, make sure it fits around the largest part of your hand.
- If you are making a bracelet, make sure to include the length of the clasp and the jump rings.

3. To make a bangle, tie the beads into a ring, and make sure it fits over your hand. Sew through a few beads to exit a Lentil. Sew through the open hole of the same Lentil. If you are making a bracelet with a clasp, end with a Lentil, and pick up seven 15ºs. Sew through the open hole of the end Lentil **(figure 2)**.

4. If you are exiting next to a 15º, pick up an 8º. If you are exiting next to an 8º, pick up a 15º. Sew through the open hole of the next Lentil. Continue, picking up the 15º or 8º needed **(figure 3)**, opposite the seed bead from the first row or round, until you complete the row or round.

5. To make a bangle, sew through the next few beads after completing the round, tying half-hitch knots, and end the working thread. (Techniques, p. 13). Remove the stop bead. Using the tail, sew though a few beads, tying half-hitch knots, and end the tail.

Tip

If you are making a bracelet with a clasp, exit the end Lentil next to the tail, and pick up seven 15⁰s. Sew through the other hole of the end Lentil and the next few beads. Tie a few half-hitch knots, and end the working thread (Techniques). Remove the stop bead. Using the tail, sew through the 15⁰s, and sew through the next few beads, tying half-hitch knots. End the tail. Attach the clasp to the end loops of seed beads using jump rings.

Design Option

Crescent and Bar beads work well in this design. You can also alternate bead colors or use fire-polished beads in place of the larger seed beads.

Brick Stitch Baby Bracelet

CREATE A TEXTURAL DELIGHT WITH BAR BEADS, LENTIL
BEADS, AND CRESCENT BEADS USING A BASIC BRICK
STITCH TECHNIQUE. YOU'LL WEAVE WITH A MIXTURE
OF CZECHMATES FOR A BRACELET WITH WONDERFUL,
DIMENSIONAL APPEAL.

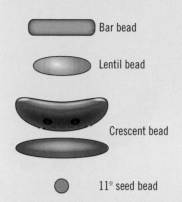

Bar bead

Lentil bead

Crescent bead

11º seed bead

CZECHMATES
Bar, Lentil, and Crescent beads

TECHNIQUES
- Adding and Ending Thread, p. 13
- Opening and Closing Jump Rings,
p. 13 (optional)
- Modified Brick Stitch, p. 13

SKILL LEVEL
Intermediate ●●●

figure 1

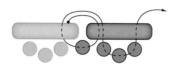

figure 2

MAKE THE BRACELET

1. Thread a needle on 4 yd. (3.7m)
of Fireline, and sew through one
hole of a Bar bead, leaving a 1-yd.
(.9m) tail. Pick up three 11º seed
beads, and sew through the other
hole of the same Bar **(figure 1)**.

2. Sew through one hole of a
new Bar and pick up an 11º. Sew
through the nearest hole of the
previous Bar and through the same
hole of the new Bar. Pick up three
11ºs, and sew through the other hole
of the new Bar **(figure 2)**. Repeat
this step until you reach the desired
length.

Tip

*To make a bangle, make sure the
strip fits around the widest part of
your hand. For a bracelet with a
clasp, keep the length of the clasp
in mind when determining the length
of the strip.*

If making a bangle, sew through the
first hole of the first Bar picked up
in the strip. Pick up an 11º, and then
sew through the same hole of the
last Bar picked up in the strip. For
a bracelet with a clasp, exit the end
hole of the last Bar picked up in
the strip.

SUPPLIES
- **92** Bar beads
- **64** Lentil beads
- **28** Crescent beads
- 6g 11º seed beads
- Fireline, 6- or 8-lb. test
- Beading needles, #12
- Clasp (optional)
- **2–4** jump rings (optional)
- **2** pairs of chainnose pliers
(optional)

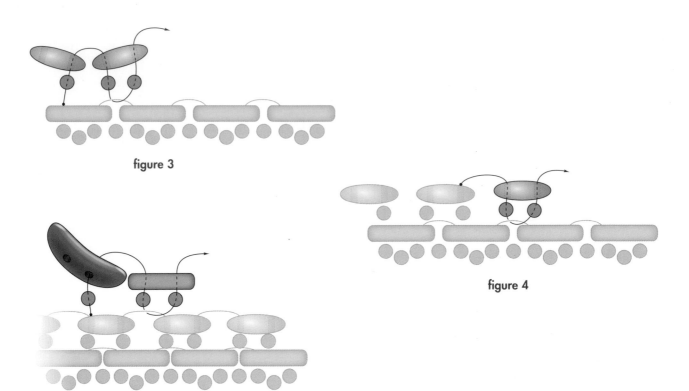

figure 3

figure 4

figure 5

3. For either bangle or bracelet, pick up an 11º, sew through one hole of two Lentil beads, and pick up an 11º. Sew under the thread bridge between the next two Bars in the previous round or row. Pick up an 11º, and sew through the open hole of the second Lentil just picked up **(figure 3)**.

4. Sew through one hole of a Lentil, pick up an 11º, and sew under the next thread bridge in the previous round or row. Pick up an 11º, and sew through the open hole of the Lentil just picked up **(figure 4)**. Repeat this step until you reach the beginning of the round or end of the row.

  If making a bangle, connect the nearest holes of the first and last Lentil in the row. For a bracelet with a clasp, exit the end hole of the last Lentil picked up.

5. Pick up an 11º, the right hole of a Crescent bead, one hole of a Bar, and an 11º. Sew under the thread bridge in the previous round or row. Pick up an 11º, and sew back through the open hole of the second Bar picked up **(figure 5)**.

6. Sew through the right hole of a Crescent, pick up an 11º, and sew under the thread bridge in the previous round. Pick up an 11º, and sew back through the open hole of the Crescent just picked up. Pick up one hole of a Bar and an 11º. Sew under the next thread bridge, pick up an 11º, and sew back through the open hole of the Bar **(figure 6)**. Repeat this step until you complete the round or row. Position the Bars to sit behind the Crescents.

7. Repeat step 6, but if making a bracelet with a clasp, pick up the Crescents through the left hole first.

8. Repeat step 6.

9. Work as in steps 3 and 4 to add a round or row of Lentils.

10. Work as in steps 3 and 4 using Bars instead of Lentils.

11. For the last round or row, exit a Bar with the needle pointing toward the edge. Pick up three 11ºs, and sew through the other hole of the same Bar, and then sew back through the nearest hole of the next Bar. Pick up an 11º, and sew back through the nearest hole of the previous Bar, and the nearest hole of the next Bar. Repeat this step **(figure 7)** until you reach the end of the row or round. Repeat along the other edge using the tail.

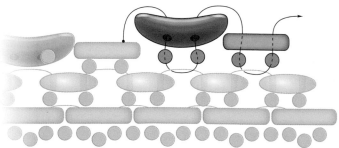

figure 6

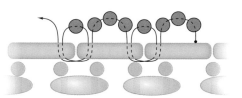

figure 7

FINISHING

If you're making a bangle, retrace the thread path of the edge 11°s. End the working thread. Repeat with the tail. If you are making a bracelet, exit the end 11° along one edge. Fill in any gaps between the last beads in every other row by picking up three or four 11°s between rows. Retrace the thread path through the edge 11°s, and add 11°s to the gaps between the last beads in every other row on this end. Retrace the thread path through the other edge 11°s, to exit next to the 11°s added along the edge. Work in modified peyote stitch (Techniques, p. 13) to strengthen the end 11°s **(figure 8)**. This will not be perfect, nor does it need to be. It just gives a bit of a foundation to add a clasp. Repeat on the other end, and have the working thread and tail exiting on opposite ends of the bracelet. Stitch the clasp in place, or attach a clasp to the openings with jump rings (Techniques).

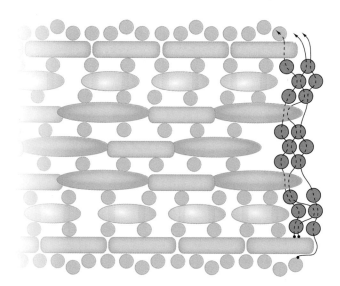

figure 8

Design Option

You can omit two of the rounds or rows of alternating Crescent beads to make a thinner bangle or bracelet. You can also substitute other two-hole beads as desired (try using Triangle beads in place of the Crescents).

Cosmic Connections Bracelet

WHETHER YOU MAKE A BANGLE OR A CLASPED VERSION, THIS BRACELET COMES TOGETHER QUICKLY. LARGE COIN PEARLS INCORPORATED INTO THE DESIGN CATCH THE EYE AND COMPLEMENT THE STITCHING.

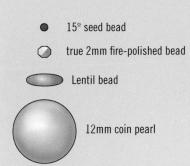

● 15º seed bead

◑ true 2mm fire-polished bead

⬭ Lentil bead

⬤ 12mm coin pearl

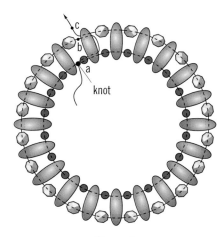

figure 1

MAKE LARGE RINGS

1. Thread a needle on 18 in. (46cm) of Fireline, and pick up a repeating pattern of a 15º seed bead and a Lentil bead 20 times, leaving a 6-in. (15cm) tail.

2. Tie the beads into a ring with a square knot (Techniques, p. 13). Sew through all the beads again, and exit through the same hole of the Lentil. Sew through the open hole of the same Lentil to change direction **(figure 1, a–b)**. Thread a needle on the tail and sew through a few beads in the inner ring. End the tail.

3. Using the working thread, pick up a true 2mm fire-polished bead, and sew through the open hole of the next Lentil in the ring. Repeat this step around the outer ring **(b–c)**, and then retrace the thread path to reinforce. Save the working thread to connect the components.

4. Make two large components. Set them aside.

CZECHMATES
Lentil or Bar beads

TECHNIQUES
- Adding and Ending Thread, p. 13
- Square Knot, p. 13
- Opening and Closing Jump Rings (optional), p. 13
- Modified Right-Angle Weave, p. 17

SKILL LEVEL
Advanced Beginner ●●○

SUPPLIES
- **6–8** 12mm coin pearls
- **120–160** true 2mm fire-polished beads
- **120–160** Lentil beads (or Bar beads)
- 3g 15º seed beads
- Fireline, 6- or 8-lb. test
- Beading needles, #12
- Multi-strand clasp (optional)
- **4** jump rings (optional)
- **2** pairs of chainnose pliers (optional)

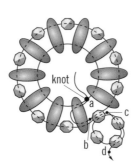

figure 2

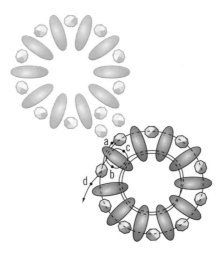

figure 3

MAKE SMALL RINGS

1. Thread a needle on 18 in. of Fireline, and pick up 10 Lentils, leaving a 6-in. tail.

2. Tie the beads into a ring with a square knot. Sew through all the beads again, and exit the same hole of the Lentil. Sew through the open hole of the same Lentil to change direction **(figure 2, a–b)**. Thread the needle on the tail and sew through a few beads in the inner ring. End the tail.

3. Pick up a true 2mm fire-polished bead, and sew through the open hole of the next Lentil in the outer ring. Repeat this step around the outer ring **(b–c)**, and then retrace the thread path to reinforce. Exit a 2mm.

4. Pick up three 2mms, and sew through the 2mm your thread exited at the start of this step. Retrace the thread path, and exit the 2mm opposite the 2mm in the initial small ring **(c–d)**.

5. Pick up a repeating pattern of a Lentil and a 2mm nine times, and then pick up a Lentil. Sew through the 2mm your thread exited at the start of this step, and the same hole of the next Lentil, maintaining a light tension **(figure 3, a–b)**. Sew through the other hole of the same Lentil to change direction. Sew through all the open holes of the Lentils to pull the center into a tight ring **(b–c)**. Sew through the Lentil and the next 2mm to exit the outer ring and end the thread **(c–d)**. Lay out the attached small rings between two large rings on your work surface.

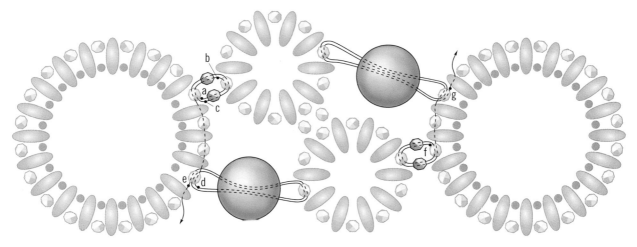

figure 4

CONNECT THE RINGS

1. Using the tail from the large ring, pick up a 2mm and sew through a 2mm along the outer edge of one of the small rings (two 2mms away from the connection of the two small rings) **(figure 4, a–b)**. Pick up a 2mm and sew through the 2mm along the outer edge of the large ring **(b–c)**. Retrace the thread path. Then sew through the beads along the outer edge of the large ring to exit two 2mms away from the connection just completed **(c–d)**.

2. Pick up a 12mm coin pearl and sew through a 2mm on the second small ring (one 2mm away from the connections of the two small rings). Sew back through the coin pearl and the 2mm along the outer edge of the large ring. Retrace the thread path **(d–e)**, and end the thread.

3. Align the next large ring and coin pearl so the spacing is the same for the first set of connections, and join them with the tail from the other large ring **(f–g)**.

4. Continue making large and small rings and connect them in the same manner until you reach the desired length.

5. Attach a clasp to the end of the rings with jump rings if desired (Techniques, p. 13), or make enough rings to fit around the largest part of your hand and stitch the ends together as for connecting the other rings.

Criss-Cross Crescents Bracelet

MAKE FUN COMPONENTS TO CREATE COLORFUL
JEWELRY FOR EVERY OUTFIT. THIS BRACELET COMPOSED
OF BEADED BEADS IS SO SIMPLE, YOU CAN MAKE MANY
DIFFERENT VERSIONS!

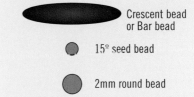

Crescent bead
or Bar bead

15º seed bead

2mm round bead

CZECHMATES:
Crescent, Bar, or Triangle beads

TECHNIQUES:
- Adding and Ending Thread, p. 13
- Modified Right-Angle Weave,
p. 17

SKILL LEVEL
Beginner ● ○ ○ ⬭

SUPPLIES PER BEADED BEAD
- **9** Crescent beads (or Bar or Triangle beads)
- **30** 15º seed beads
- **6** 2mm round crystals or true 2mm fire-polished beads
- Fireline, 6-lb. test
- Beading needles, #12

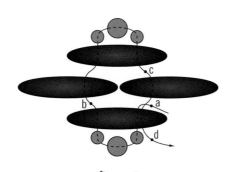

figure 1

MAKE THE BEADED BEAD

1. Lay out three Crescent beads
on your work surface so the points
are facing up as if smiling at you.
(Check both holes as you pick up
the beads, and discard any beads
with blocked holes.)

2. Thread a needle on 24 in.
(61cm) of Fireline, and sew through
the right hole of a Crescent from
the top down, leaving a 6-in. (15cm)
tail. Pick up a 15º seed bead, a 2mm
bead, and a 15º. Sew through the
other hole of the same Crescent
from the bottom up **(figure 1, a–b).**

3. Sew through the right hole of a
new Crescent from the top down.
Sew through the left hole of a new
Crescent from the top down. Pick
up a 15º, a 2mm, and a 15º, and sew
down through the other hole of the
same Crescent just picked up **(b–c).**

4. Sew through the left hole of a
new Crescent from top down. Sew
through the right hole of the first
Crescent picked up in step 2, where
the tail is exiting **(c–d)**. Retrace
the thread path to hold the beads
together.

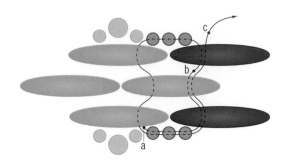

figure 2

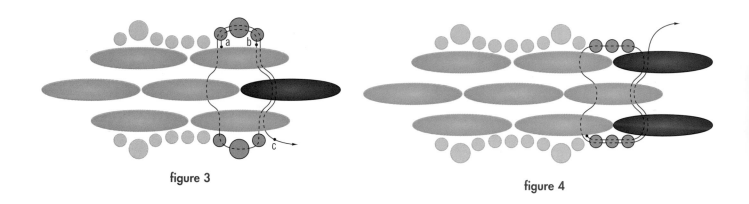

figure 3

figure 4

5. Pick up three 15ºs, and sew through the left hole of a new Crescent from the top down. Sew through the open hole of the nearest center Crescent **(figure 2, a–b)**.

6. Sew through the left hole of a new Crescent bead from top down, and pick up three 15ºs. Sew through the nearest three holes of the previous three Crescents, the three 15ºs, and the three holes of the two newest and center Crescents **(b–c)**.

7. Pick up a 15º, a 2mm, and a 15º **(figure 3, a–b)**, and sew through the open hole of the Crescent your thread is exiting. Sew through the

right hole of a new Crescent, and the open hole of the next Crescent. Pick up a 15º, a 2mm, and a 15º, and sew through the three holes of the previous three Crescents, and the first 15º, 2mm, and 15º picked up in this step. Sew through the three holes of the next three Crescents **(b–c)**.

8. Repeat steps 5 and 6 **(figure 4)**.

9. Pick up a 15º, a 2mm, and a 15º, and sew through the open hole of the Crescent your thread is exiting, the open hole of the first center bead, and the open hole of the remaining Crescent **(figure 5, a–b)**. Pick up a 15º, a 2mm, and a 15º, and sew through the three holes of the previous three Crescents **(b–c)**. Retrace the thread path to reinforce.

10. Pick up three 15ºs in the open spaces along each edge of the bead. Sew through the rings of seed beads along each edge of the beaded bead, and end the threads (Techniques, p. 13).

11. Make the desired number of beads. Slide the beads on a finished bracelet.

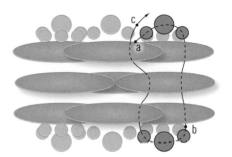

figure 5

Design Option

Make earrings: Cut two 3-in. (7.6cm) pieces of chain. Slide a bead on a chain, and attach the end links with a jump ring (Techniques, p. 13). Attach an earring finding to the jump ring. You can also use Bar or Triangle beads to make the beaded beads.

Curly Q Necklace

USE A SIMPLE STRINGING TECHNIQUE TO CREATE A CURLY, TWIRLY BRACELET OR NECKLACE. THIS PRETTY PIECE COULDN'T BE EASIER! IT'S THE PERFECT ACCESSORY FOR A CASUAL OUTFIT.

 Lentil bead

 11º seed bead

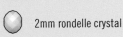 2mm rondelle crystal

CZECHMATES
Lentil or Bar beads

TECHNIQUES
- Crimping, p. 13
- Opening and Closing Jump Rings, p. 13

SKILL LEVEL
Beginner ⬤◯◯

SUPPLIES
- **340** Lentil beads, or approximately 20 beads per inch
- **339** 2mm rondelle crystals
- 5 ft. (1.5m) beading wire, size .012-.015
- **9** 11º seed beads
- **1** crimp bead
- **2** Bead Stoppers (not stop beads)
- **2** 4–6mm jump rings
- 2-part clasp
- **2** pairs of chainnose pliers
- Crimping pliers
- Wire cutters

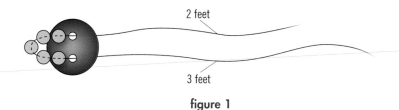

2 feet

3 feet

figure 1

MAKE THE NECKLACE

1. Attach a Bead Stopper 2 ft. (61cm) from the end of 5 ft. (1.5m) of beading wire. On the shorter wire, pick up five 11º seed beads and a Lentil bead. Keeping the beads at the 2-ft. mark, remove the Bead Stopper, and go through the open hole of the Lentil with the longer wire **(figure 1)**. Reposition the Bead Stopper over the longer wire to hold the beads in place.

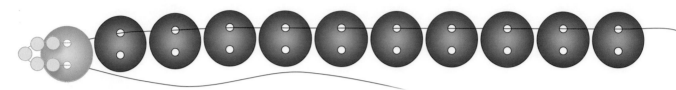

figure 2

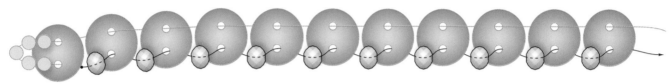

figure 3

2. On the shorter wire, pick up ten Lentils **(figure 2)**. Reposition the Bead Stopper to hold the ten new Lentils in place.

3. With the longer wire, pick up a 2mm rondelle and go through the open hole of the next Lentil. Repeat to add a 2mm between each remaining open hole **(figure 3)**, while shaping the Lentils into a curve. Reposition the Bead Stopper to hold both wires.

4. Repeat steps 2 and 3 until you reach the desired length.

Tip
The tighter you pull, the tighter the curl will be.

5. Ending with a Lentil over both strands, pick up two 11ºs on each wire. Pick up a crimp bead on one strand and string the other strand through the crimp bead in the opposite direction, crossing the wires. Crimp the crimp bead (Techniques, p. 13) and trim the tails.

6. Attach a clasp to both 11º seed bead loops with jump rings (Techniques).

Design Option

To make a necklace, attach a piece of chain to both 11º seed bead loops with jump rings, and then attach a clasp half to each end link of the chains with jump rings.

DiamonDuo Bangle

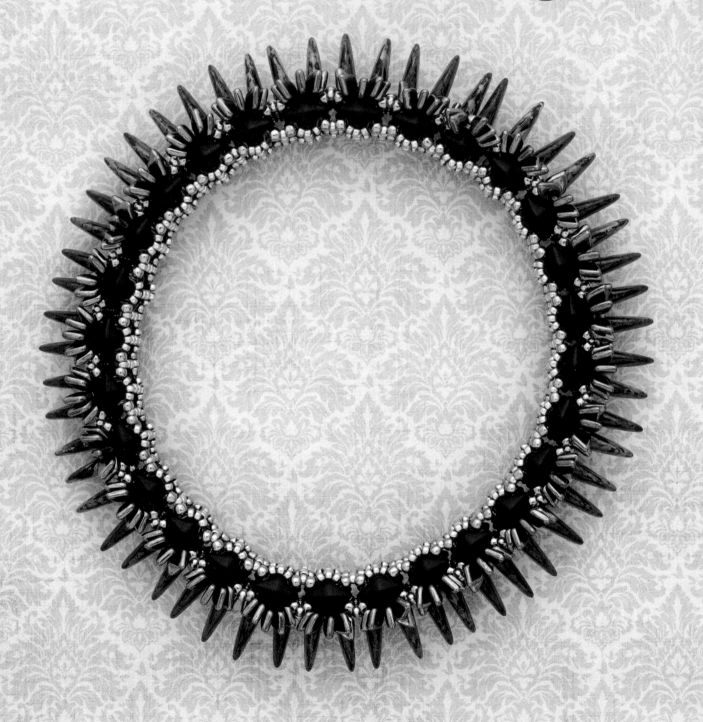

TWO-HOLE DAGGER BEADS AND DIAMONDUO BEADS CREATE A SUBSTANTIAL BASE FOR LOADS OF LOVELY EMBELLISHMENTS, BUT THE POSITION OF THE DAGGER BEADS GIVE THIS BANGLE A BIT OF A DANGEROUS EDGE.

Dagger bead

DiamonDuo bead

 3mm bead

Dragon scale bead

 11º seed bead

15º seed bead

figure 1

MAKE THE BANGLE

1. Thread a needle on each end of 3 yd. (2.7m) of Fireline. Sew through the top hole of a Dagger bead, and center it on the thread.

2. Lay out the DiamonDuos flat side down, and holes facing north to south. Check all the holes to make sure they are not blocked.

3. With one needle, pick up a DiamonDuo through the right hole, sew through the bottom hole of the same Dagger, pick up a Diamon-Duo through the right hole, and sew through the top hole of the same Dagger **(figure 1)**. With the other thread, sew through all the beads so the threads are exiting opposite sides of the top hole of the Dagger (you are sandwiching the Dagger between the DiamonDuos, which are facing out).

CZECHMATES
Dagger beads

TECHNIQUES
- Adding and Ending Thread, p. 13
- Modified Right-Angle Weave, p. 17

SKILL LEVEL
Intermediate ⬤ ⬤ ⬭

SUPPLIES
- **54–60** DiamonDuos
- **54–60** Dagger beads
- 4g 11º seed beads
- 6g 15º seed beads
- **550–600** dragon scale beads
- **110–120** 3mm round beads
- Fireline, 6- or 8-lb. test
- **2** beading needles, #12

4. With each needle, pick up a 3mm round bead, and cross the needles through the top hole of a new Dagger **(figure 2)**. With each needle, pick up five dragon scale beads, and cross through the top hole of the previous Dagger **(figure 3)**. With each needle, retrace the thread path through the dragon scale beads, and cross through the top hole of the new Dagger.

5. With one needle, sew down through the open hole of the DiamonDuo, the bottom hole of the Dagger, and then sew up through the open hole of the opposite DiamonDuo, the top hole of the same Dagger, and the same hole of the DiamonDuo. With the other needle, retrace the thread path in the opposite direction, so both threads exit the bottom of the DiamonDuos.

6. With the right needle, pick up an 11º seed bead, a 15º seed bead, an 11º, and the left hole of a Diamon-Duo. Pick up an 11º, a 15º, and an 11º, and sew through the hole of the DiamonDuo your thread exited at the start of this step. Retrace the thread path, skipping the center 15ºs, to pull the beads into a point. Sew through the beadwork to exit the center 15º at the top **(figure 4)**.

7. Add a second DiamonDuo to the other side, following essentially the same instructions as in step 6: With the left needle, pick up an 11º, a 15º, an 11º, and the right hole of a DiamonDuo. Pick up an 11º, a 15º, an 11º, and sew through the hole of the DiamonDuo your thread exited at the start of this step. Retrace the thread path, skipping the center 15º, to pull the beads into a point. Sew through the beadwork to exit the center 15º at the top.

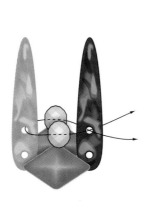

figure 2

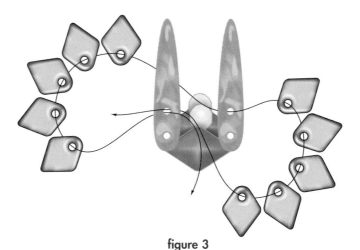

figure 3

8. With one needle, pick up four 15°s, and sew through the opposite 15° along the other edge of the beadwork. Sew back through the four 15°s just picked up, the 15° you exited at the start of this step, the next 11°, and the nearest hole of the previous DiamonDuo (**figure 5, top view**). Sew through the bottom 11°, and exit the bottom 15°. Pick up two 11°s, and sew through the 15° along the opposite edge, back through the two 11°s just pick up, the 15° along this edge, and the next 11°. Exit the nearest hole of the new DiamonDuo (**figure 5, bottom view**). With the other needle, retrace the thread path to exit the same hole of the other DiamonDuo.

9. With one needle, sew through the top hole of a new Dagger, and sew through the same hole of the DiamonDuo along the opposite edge, the bottom hole of the same Dagger, up through the same hole of the DiamonDuo along this edge, and through the top hole of the same Dagger (see **figure 1** for thread path). Retrace the thread path with the other needle to exit the top hole on the opposite side of the same Dagger.

10. Repeat steps 4–9 until you reach the desired length, adding and ending thread as needed (Techniques, p. 13).

11. To end the bangle, finish with step 6, but don't pick up a new DiamonDuo. Instead, join the first and last DiamonDuos with an 11°, 15°, and 11° along each end. Then continue as in step 6.

top view

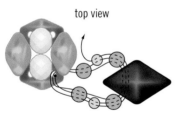

figure 4

top view

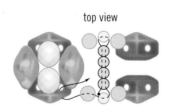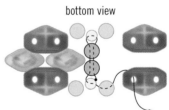

bottom view

figure 5

Emerald City Beaded Bead

THE CONSTRUCTION OF THIS BEADED BEAD RESULTS IN A
LOVELY, PEBBLED-BRICK LOOK. IT'S QUICK AND EASY, SO TRY
MAKING MULTIPLE BEADS IN A FEW DIFFERENT COLORS FOR
JEWELRY THAT MATCHES ANY OUTFIT.

 11º seed bead

 2mm rondelle crystal

Tile bead

CZECHMATES
Tile or Brick beads

TECHNIQUES
- Adding and Ending Thread, p. 13
- Modified Right-Angle Weave,
p. 17

SKILL LEVEL
Advanced Beginner

SUPPLIES PER BEADED BEAD
- **8** Tile beads
- **16** 11º seed beads
- **16** 2mm rondelle crystals
- Fireline, 6- or 8-lb. test
- Beading needles, #12
- Finished bracelet chain

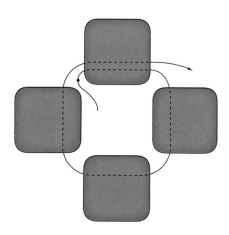

figure 1

1. Thread a needle on 1 yd. (.9m) of Fireline, and pick up four Tile beads, leaving a 6-in. (15cm) tail. Sew through all the beads again to form a ring, and then sew through the same hole of the first Tile again **(figure 1)**.

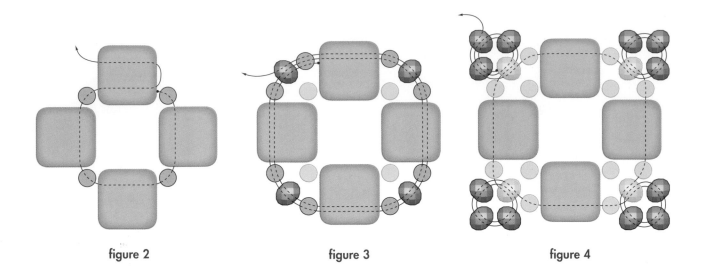

figure 2

figure 3

figure 4

2. Pick up an 11º seed bead, and sew through the same hole of the next Tile. Repeat three times, exiting the first Tile. Sew through the other hole of the same Tile to change direction **(figure 2)**.

3. Pick up an 11º, a 2mm rondelle crystal, and an 11º, and sew through the open hole of the next Tile. Repeat three times, retrace the thread path, and exit the first 2mm **(figure 3)**.

4. Pick up three 2mms, sew through the same 2mm your thread exited at the start of this step, retrace the thread path, and sew through the next four beads to exit the next 2mm. Repeat three times, and then sew through the first two 2mms picked up in this step **(figure 4)**.

BEADED BEAD SIDE VIEW

5. Pick up an 11º, a new Tile, and an 11º. Sew through the corresponding 2mm in the next unit of 2mms. Repeat three times, and then retrace the thread path, exiting the same hole of the first Tile picked up in this step. Sew through the open hole of the same Tile to change direction **(figure 5)**.

6. Sew through the open hole of the next Tile. Repeat three times to close up the bead. Pick up an 11º, and sew through the same hole of the next Tile. Repeat three times, and retrace the thread path. End the working thread and tail (Techniques, p. 13).

7. Repeat steps 1–6 to make additional beads as desired. Slide the beaded beads over a finished chain.

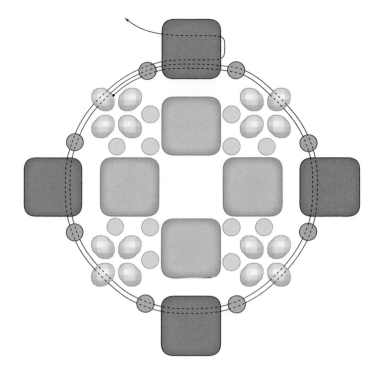

figure 5

Design Option

Make the desired number of beads for a necklace or pair of earrings. You can also make the beaded beads with Brick beads.

Irresistibangle

STACK BAR BEADS TO CREATE COLORFUL COMPONENTS WITHIN THIS WOVEN BANGLE OF SPARKLING CRYSTALS AND SEED BEADS. YOU'LL LOVE THE HEFT AND FEEL OF THIS SUBSTANTIAL PIECE.

CZECHMATES:
Bar, Triangle, or Brick beads

TECHNIQUES:
- Adding and Ending Thread, p. 13
- Netting, p. 15
- Modified Chevron Chain, p. 15

SKILL LEVEL:
Advanced Beginner ● ● ○

SUPPLIES
- Bar beads
  - **160** color A
  - **80** color B
- **160** 4mm bicone crystals
- 5g 11º seed beads
- Fireline, 6- or 8-lb. test
- Beading needles, #12

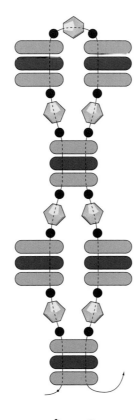

figure 1

MAKE THE BANGLE

1. Thread a needle and attach a stop bead to the center of 4 yd. (3.8m) of Fireline.

2. Pick up the left hole of a color A Bar bead, a color B Bar bead, and an A. Pick up an 11º seed bead, a 4mm crystal, and an 11º. Pick up the right hole of an A, a B, and an A. Pick up an 11º, a 4mm, and an 11º. Repeat this step once, and then pick up the left hole of an A, a B, and an A, an 11º, a 4mm, and an 11º. Skip the last 15 beads, and sew through the open holes of the next three Bars.

3. Pick up an 11º, a 4mm, an 11º, the left holes of an A, B, and A, an 11º, a 4mm, and an 11º. Skip the next nine beads, and sew through the open holes of the original three Bars **(figure 1)**.

4. Pick up an 11º, a 4mm, an 11º, the right holes of an A, B, and A, an 11º, a 4mm, and an 11º. Skip nine beads, and sew through the open holes of the next three Bars **(figure 2)**. Repeat **(figure 3)**.

5. Repeat steps 3 and 4 until you reach your desired length.

6. Connect the ends: Pick up an 11º, a 4mm, and an 11º. Sew through the open holes of the corresponding A, B, and A from the first row. Pick up an 11º, a 4mm, and an 11º. Sew through the open holes of the corresponding A, B, and A from the last row. Pick up an 11º, a 4mm, and an 11º. Sew through the open holes of the corresponding A, B, and A from the first row. Pick up an 11º, a 4mm, and an 11º. Sew through the open holes of the corresponding A, B, and A from the last row. Pick up an 11º, a 4mm, and an 11º. Sew through the left holes of the corresponding A, B, and A from the first row **(figure 4)**. Retrace the thread path to reinforce the join, and then end the working thread (Techniques, p. 13).

7. With the remaining thread, sew through the nearest 11º, 4mm, and 11º along one edge. Pick up two 11ºs, and sew through the next 11º, 4mm, and 11º along this edge. Repeat to the end. Sew through the beadwork to reach the other edge.

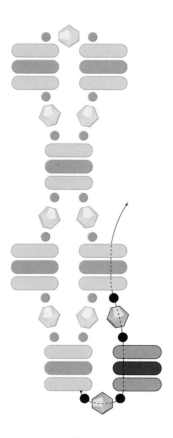

figure 2

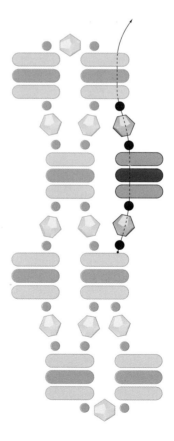

figure 3

Repeat along this edge, and then end the thread. (To achieve the right fit, check the bracelet against your wrist when you reach the final row, holding it loosely. The last seed bead row tightens the stitching and doesn't allow for much stretch.)

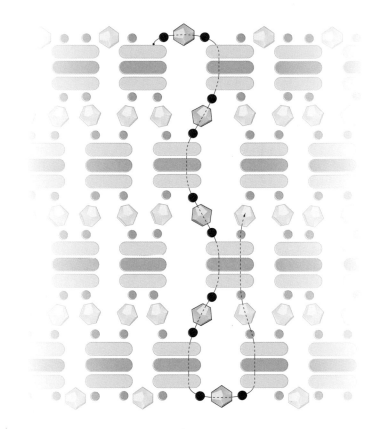

figure 4

Design Option

Try using only one Bar bead instead of three for a thinner bangle.

Juxtaposition Bangle

SINGLE LAYERS JOINED WITH RIGHT-ANGLE WEAVE
UNITS COULD CREATE A SUBSTANTIAL STACKED PIECE.
TO BEGIN, STICK WITH TWO STACKS FOR A PAIRED-DOWN
CLOVER-SHAPED BANGLE.

Crescent bead

3-4mm bead

2-3mm bead

CZECHMATES
Bar, Lentil, or Crescent beads

TECHNIQUES
- Adding and Ending Thread, p. 13
- Right-Angle Weave, p. 17

SKILL LEVEL
Intermediate

SUPPLIES
- **60** Crescent beads per stack
- **60** 3–4mm crystals or pearls
- **60** 2–3mm pearls or rondelle crystals
- **48** extra 2–4mm beads to connect layers
- Fireline, 6- or 8-lb. test
- Beading needles, #13 or #11

MAKE THE BANGLE

1. Thread a needle and attach a stop bead to the center of a 2-yd. (1.8m) length of Fireline.

2. If using Bar beads or Lentil beads, just alternate a 2–3mm bead and a Bar five times, then a 3–4mm bead and a Bar nine times **(figure 1)**, and repeat four times. (You may need to adjust the length to fit for a bangle, but once you figure out that first layer, you can make the rest with little aggravation.)

Tip
If you are using Crescent beads, as in my example, pick up the Crescents the same way each time. Lay the Crescents out on your work surface, and pick up the same hole each time for the first inner round.

figure 1

figure 2

3. Sew through the same hole of the last Bar to form a ring. Sew through the other hole of the same Bar to change direction. If you are exiting next to the 2–3mm bead, pick up a 3–4mm bead, and vice versa **(figure 2)**. This allows the beadwork to curve nicely. Repeat around the ring, adding the opposite bead between each Bar by picking up a bead and sewing through the open hole of the next Bar.

Tip
With steps 1–3, don't reinforce the beadwork until after connecting the layers together. Otherwise, it is difficult to get through the beadwork.

4. After completing step 3, set this layer aside, and make another one by repeating steps 1–3.

5. Connecting the layers is easy: Just locate the center points of the inner ring of one of the layers in the section of five alternating Bar and 2–3mm beads. Remove the stop bead, and exit the center 2–3mm bead. Pick up any bead or combination of beads just picked up. For example, you may pick up a 2mm, a 3mm, and a 2mm, stack the layers, and then sew through the corresponding bead in another

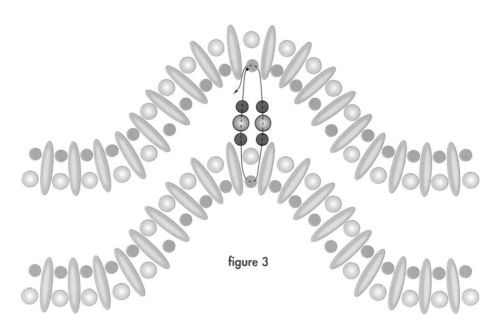

figure 3

layer **(figure 3)**. Retrace the thread path to reinforce the join, and then sew through the inner ring of the first layer to the next connection point. Connect the remaining points along the inner layer, and then sew through the beadwork to exit the outer layer, and connect the layers in the same manner. End the working thread and tail.

Design Option

Make two sets of layers or more, and then connect the sets for a wide bangle.

On the Edge
Bracelet

WEAVE A LOVELY TAPESTRY OF TWO-HOLE BEADS AND O-BEADS, CREATING A BEAUTIFUL ACCESSORY FOR ANY OCCASION. A FEW CRYSTALS SCATTERED ON THE EDGES OFFERS A LITTLE SPARKLE, TOO!

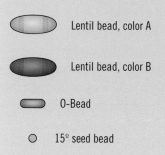

Lentil bead, color A

Lentil bead, color B

O-Bead

15º seed bead

CZECHMATES
Lentil or Bar beads

TECHNIQUES
- Adding and Ending Thread, p. 13
- Opening and Closing Jump Rings, p. 13
- Modified Chevron Chain, p. 15

SKILL LEVEL
Beginner ● ○ ○

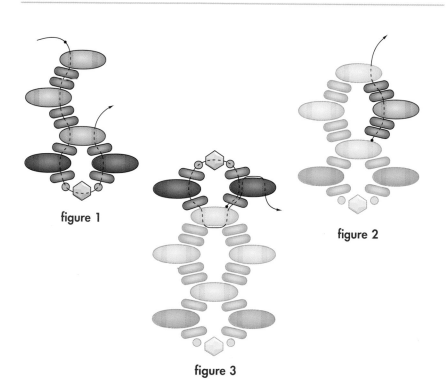

figure 1

figure 2

figure 3

SUPPLIES
- Lentil beads
  - **66** color A
  - **44** color B
- **352** O-Beads
- **36** 3mm bicone crystals
- **2g** 15º seed beads
- Fireline, 8-lb. test
- Beading needles, #12
- 2-strand clasp (optional)
- **4** jump rings (optional)
- **2** pairs of chainnose pliers (optional)

BEGIN THE BRACELET

1. Thread a needle on 3 yd. (2.7m) of Fireline, and pick up the following beads, leaving a 12-in. (30cm) tail: A color A Lentil bead, two O-Beads, an A, two O-Beads, an A, an O-Bead, a color B Lentil bead, an O-Bead, a 15º seed bead, a 3mm bicone crystal, a 15º, an O-Bead, a B, and an O-Bead. Skip the last nine beads picked up, and sew back through the other hole of the next A **(figure 1)**.

2. Pick up two O-Beads, an A, and two O-Beads. Skip five beads, and sew through the open hole of the next A **(figure 2)**.

3. Pick up an O-Bead, a B, an O-Bead, a 15º, a 3mm, a 15º, an O-Bead, a B, and an O-Bead. Sew through the other hole of the A your thread is exiting. Sew through the other hole of the same A, the next O-Bead, and the same hole of the following B. Sew through the open hole of the same B to change direction **(figure 3)**.

4. Pick up an O-Bead, an A, and two O-Beads. Skip four beads, and sew through the open hole of the next A. Pick up two O-Beads, an A, and an O-Bead. Skip four beads, and sew through the open hole of the next B (**figure 4**).

5. Pick up an O-Bead, a 15º, a 3mm, a 15º, an O-Bead, a B, and an O-Bead. Skip the last seven beads just picked up and two beads in the previous row. Sew back through the open hole of the next A (**figure 5**).

6. Pick up two O-Beads, an A, and two O-Beads. Skip five beads, and sew through the open hole of the next A (**figure 6**).

7. Pick up an O-Bead, a B, an O-Bead, a 15º, a 3mm, a 15º, and an O-Bead. Sew through the open hole of the previous B along this edge, the next O-Bead, and the same hole of the following A. Sew through the other hole of the same A, the next O-Bead, and the same hole of the next B. Sew through the open hole of the same B to change direction (**figure 7**).

8. Repeat steps 4–7 until you reach the desired length.

MAKE A BRACELET WITH A CLASP

End after completing step 7. Pick up five 15ºs, and sew through the open hole of the next A. Pick up five 15ºs, and sew through the open hole of the next B. Pick up a 15º, and sew back through all the beads until you sew through the B on the other edge. Pick up a 15º, and sew back through the B (**figure 8**). Retrace all the beads again, and then end the working thread. Repeat with the tail. Attach a two-strand clasp to the ends using jump rings (Techniques, p. 13).

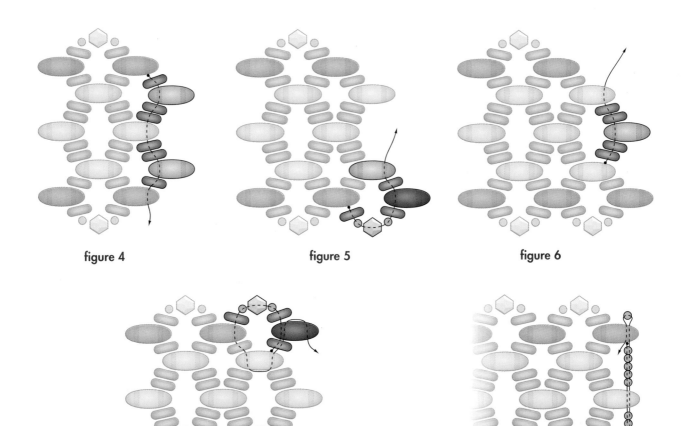

figure 4   figure 5   figure 6

figure 7   figure 8

Design Option

Make a cuff or a bangle.
Either choice works nicely
with this design.

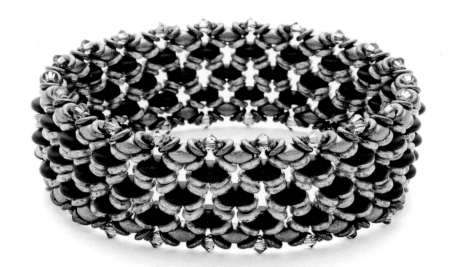

MAKE A BANGLE

End after completing step 4. Pick up an O-Bead, a 15º, a 3mm, a 15º, and an O-Bead. Sew through the open hole of the first B in the first row. Pick up an O-Bead, and sew through the open hole of the next A in the last row. Pick up two O-Beads, and sew through the open hole of the next A in the first row. Pick up two O-Beads, and sew through the open hole of the next A in the last row. Pick up an O-Bead and sew through the open hole of the next B in the first row. Pick up an O-Bead, a 15º, a 3mm, a 15º, and an O-Bead. Sew through the open hole of the B along the same edge **(figure 9)**. Retrace the thread path through the end rows to reinforce the join, and then end the working thread and tail (Techniques).

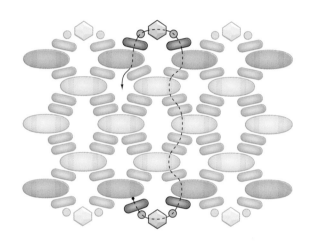

figure 9

Color Option

Peyote Petals Pendant

PEYOTE-STITCH PETALS AND A QUADRATILE CENTER COME TOGETHER IN THIS EASY, ELEGANT PENDANT. STRING ON A SIMPLE NECK CHAIN FOR EFFORTLESS ELEGANCE.

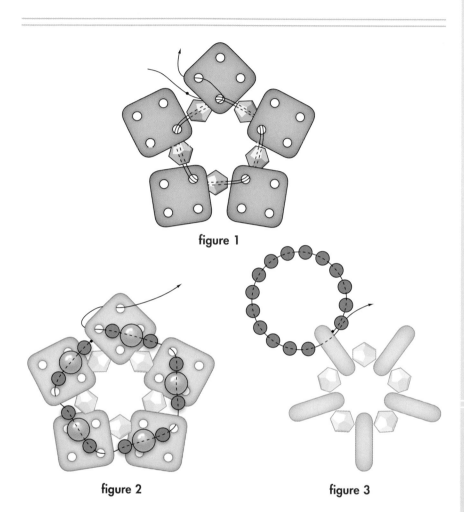

figure 1

figure 2

figure 3

11º seed bead, color A

11º seed bead, color B

3mm bicone crystal

3mm pearl

3mm fire-polished bead

QuadraTile bead

(side view)

CZECHMATES
QuadraTile or QuadraLentil beads

TECHNIQUES
- Adding and Ending Thread, p. 13
- Peyote Stitch, p. 16

SKILL LEVEL
Advanced Beginner ●●○

SUPPLIES
- **5** QuadraTile or QuadraLentil beads
- 11º seed beads
  - 2g color A
  - 2g color B
- **5** 3mm bicone or rondelle crystals
- **5** 3mm pearls or other round beads
- **5** 3mm fire-polished beads
- Fireline, 6-lb. test
- Beading needles, #12
- Finished necklace or chain

MAKE THE PENDANT

1. Thread a needle and center a repeating pattern of a 3mm crystal and one hole of a QuadraTile bead five times on 3 yd. (2.7m) of Fireline. Sew through all the same holes again, and exit next to the tail. Tie the working thread and tail together, and then exit the same hole of a QuadraTile. Sew through the adjacent hole of the same bead to change direction **(figure 1)**.

2. Pick up a color A 11º, a 3mm pearl, and an A. Sew through the corresponding hole of the next QuadraTile. Repeat to complete the round. Sew through the adjacent hole of the bead your thread is exiting to change direction **(figure 2)**.

3. (The second round is not shown for clarity.) Pick up 15 color A 11º seed beads, and sew through the same hole of the same QuadraTile your thread exited at the start of this step, and the following A **(figure 3)**.

4. Work a round of peyote off the loop of As picked up in step 3 by picking up an A, skipping an A, and sewing through the next A (Techniques, p. 13). Repeat around the loop until you sew through the last A. Sew through the same hole of the QuadraTile, and pick up an A, a 3mm fire-polished bead, and an A. Sew through the corresponding hole of the next QuadraTile **(figure 4)**.

5. Repeat steps 3 and 4 to create a peyote loop off of each QuadraTile.

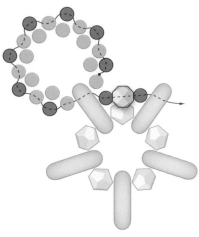

figure 4

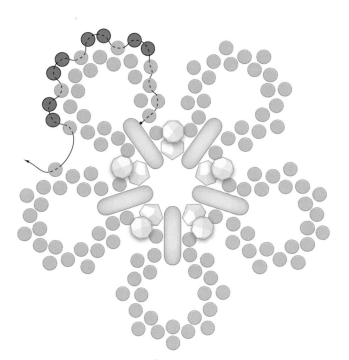

figure 5

6. Sew through the first four As in the first petal in this round, and work the next four stitches using two color B 11º seed beads per stitch. Sew through the corresponding A on the next petal **(figure 5)**.

7. Work four stitches using two Bs per stitch and the corresponding A in the next petal. Repeat this step three more times, and then sew through the corresponding A from the first petal. Sew through the beadwork to exit the same hole of any QuadraTile in this round, and then sew through the remaining hole of the same QuadraTile to change direction.

8. Pick up two Bs, an A, 12 Bs, an A, and a B. Skip the last B, and sew back through the next A. Pick up 12 Bs, and sew through the next A picked up in the first part of this step. Pick up two Bs, and then sew through the remaining hole of the next QuadraTile. Repeat four times **(figure 6)**. Sew through the beadwork to end the thread in the previous layer of petals (Techniques).

9. Thread a needle on the tail. Sew through the nearest hole of the next QuadraTile, and then sew through the adjacent hole of the same QuadraTile to exit next to the new petal of Bs. Sew through the first two Bs and following A **(figure 7, point A)**.

PENDANT SIDE

10. Work five peyote stitches using Bs off the first edge of 12 Bs **(figure 7, a–b)**. Work one stitch by picking up a B, an A, and a B, skipping six beads at the top of the petal, and sewing through the next B along the other edge of 12 Bs **(b–c)**. Work the next five stitches using Bs, exiting the A at the bottom of the petal and the following B **(c–d)**. Work five stitches using As, but sew through the first B picked up at the top of the petal, skip the A, and sew through the next B **(d–e)**. Work five stitches using As along this edge, and then sew through the beadwork to exit the A at the bottom of the next petal **(e–f)**. Repeat this step to complete the pendant. End the thread.

11. Hang the pendant from a finished chain.

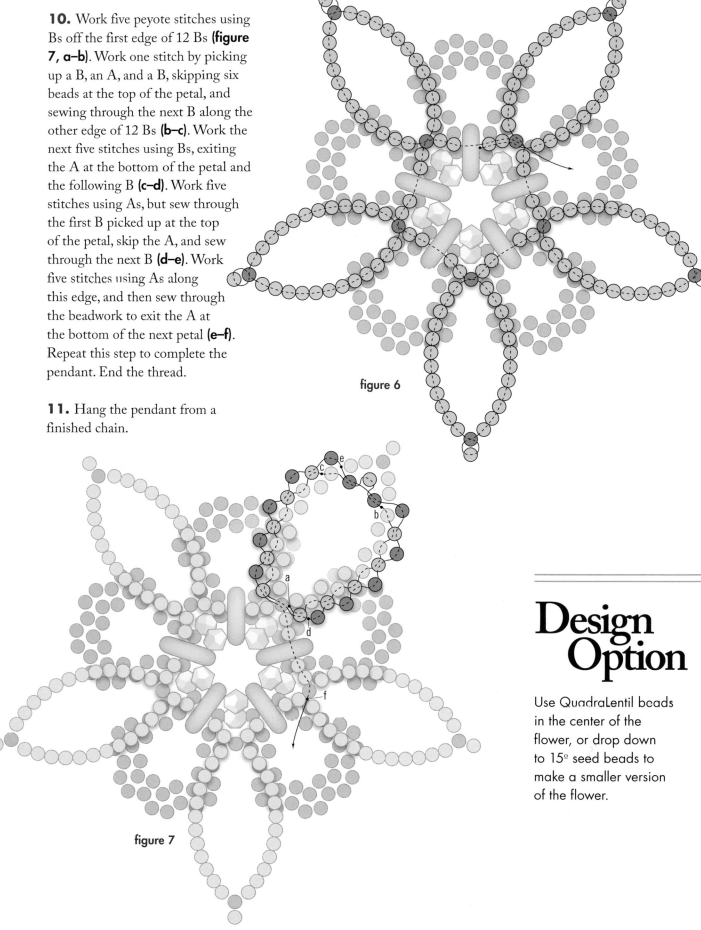

figure 6

figure 7

Design Option

Use QuadraLentil beads in the center of the flower, or drop down to 15º seed beads to make a smaller version of the flower.

Quad Stackers Bangle

STRING UP AN UNDULATING BANGLE USING A SIMPLE TECHNIQUE, BUT BULK IT UP BY USING ALL THE HOLES OF THE QUADRATILE OR LENTIL BEADS, PACKING IN THE CRYSTALS AND BEADS. THIS FUN BANGLE WILL HAVE YOU WANTING TO MAKE SEVERAL TO STACK UP ON YOUR WRIST.

QuadraTile bead

3mm crystal or pearl

2.1x2mm rondelle or true 2mm fire polished bead

8mm bead

MAKE THE BANGLE

1. Thread a needle on a doubled 3–4 yd. (2.7–3.6m) length of Fireline, and condition the thread with microcrystalline wax.

2. Pick up a repeating pattern of the following beads, leaving a 6-in. (15cm) tail: * a 3mm round bead and a QuadraLentil bead five times * a 2mm rondelle or true 2mm and a QuadraLentil seven times **(figure 1)**.

3. Repeat step 2 five more times until you have six sections of 2mms and 3mms.

4. Tie the working thread and tail together with a surgeon's knot or square knot (Techniques, p. 13), and sew through the first five 3mms and QuadraLentil picked up, exiting a QuadraLentil. Sew through the adjacent hole of the QuadraLentil, back through the same hole your thread just exited, and through the adjacent hole of the QuadraLentil again. This locks the thread in place; do this at the end of each section.

5. Pick up a 3mm, and sew through the corresponding hole of the next QuadraLentil. Repeat four more times to add a 3mm next to each 3mm in the previous round. Lock the thread in place as in step 4.

CZECHMATES
QuadraTile or QuadraLentil beads

TECHNQUES
- Adding and Ending Thread, p. 13
- Conditioning Thread, p. 13
- Surgeon's Knot or Square Knot, p. 13

SKILL LEVEL
Beginner ●○○

SUPPLIES
- **60** QuadraTile or QuadraLentil beads
- **6** 8mm round beads or pearls
- **168** 3mm round beads
- **144** 2.1x2mm rondelle crystals
- Fireline, 6- or 8-lb. test
- Beading needles, #12
- Microcrystalline wax

figure 1

6. Pick up a 2mm, and sew through the corresponding hole of the next QuadraLentil. Repeat six more times to add a 2mm next to each 2mm in the previous round. Lock the thread in place as in step 4.

7. Alternate between 2 and 3mms to add the corresponding bead to each section and lock the thread in place after each section, except in the last section. Lock the thread in place by sewing through an adjacent hole of the QuadraLentil your thread is exiting, and through the hole in the previous round. The two previous rounds will make up the inner round of the bangle. Sew through an open hole to bring the thread to the outer edge.

8. Where there are 3mms, fill in the spaces with 2mms and where there are 2mms, fill the spaces with 3mms **(figure 2)**, sewing through the corresponding holes of the QuadraLentils and locking the thread in place as in the inner round. The bracelet will begin to curve into the desired shape. Complete this round, and then sew through the remaining outer hole of the QuadraLentil. Work another outer round to match the previous outer round, locking the thread in place.

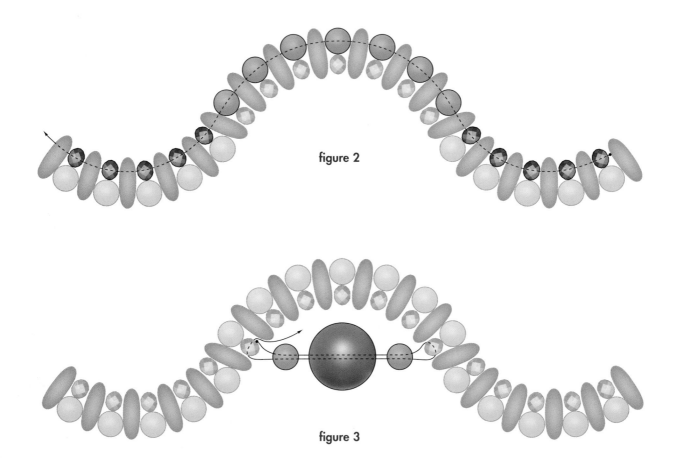

figure 2

figure 3

9. Exit the first 2mm of a section along the inner round, and pick up a 3mm, an 8mm bead, and a 3mm. Sew through the 2mm at the end of this section, and then sew back through the 3mm, 8mm, and 3mm just picked up. Sew through the same 2mm at the beginning of this section **(figure 3)**. Sew through the first 3mm and 8mm again. Pick up a 3mm, and sew through the adjacent 2mm at the end of this section. Sew

back through the 3mm just picked up and the 8mm. Pick up a 3mm and sew through the adjacent 2mm at the start of this section. Sew through the beads along the inner round to exit the first 2mm in the next section of 2mms. Repeat this step five times, and then end the working thread and tail (Techniques, p. 13).

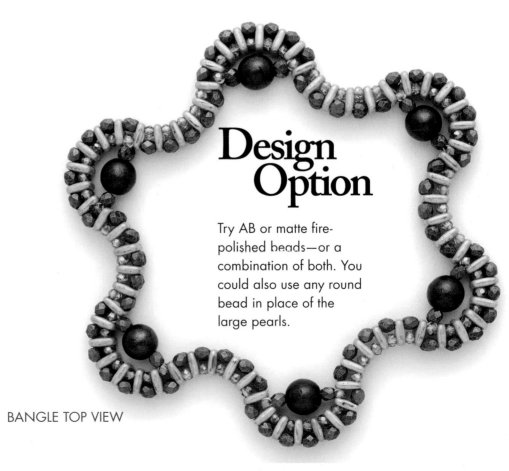

Design Option

Try AB or matte fire-polished beads—or a combination of both. You could also use any round bead in place of the large pearls.

BANGLE TOP VIEW

Quadra Cool Bracelet

OFFSET UNITS OF CRYSTALS, SNUGGED UP BETWEEN
LAYERS OF QUADRATILE BEADS, TO CREATE A UNIQUE
BRACELET OR NECKLACE.

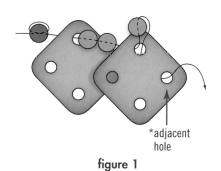

*adjacent
hole

figure 1

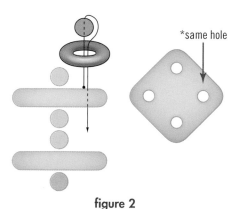

*same hole

figure 2

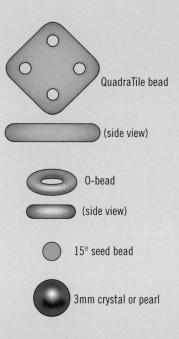

QuadraTile bead

(side view)

O-bead

(side view)

15º seed bead

3mm crystal or pearl

CZECHMATES
QuadraTile or Bar beads (for a
bracelet half the width)

TECHNIQUES
- Adding and Ending Thread, p. 13
- Stop Bead, p. 13
- Opening and Closing Jump Rings,
p. 13

SKILL LEVEL
Intermediate ● ● ●

SUPPLIES
- **44** QuadraTile beads
- **88** O-Beads
- **33** 3mm crystals or pearls
- 3g 15º seed beads
- Fireline, 6- or 8-lb. test
- Beading needle, #12
- Clasp
- **4** 4–6mm jump rings
- **2** pairs of chainnose pliers

Note: These quantites make one
bracelet. Triple the quantities for
a necklace.

MAKE THE FIRST UNIT

1. Thread a needle on 3 yd. (2.7m)
of Fireline, and pick up a stop bead,
leaving a 12-in. (30cm) tail. Pick up
a QuadraTile bead, two 15º seed
beads, a QuadraTile, and a 15º. Skip
the last 15º, and sew back through
the same hole of the nearest QuadraTile. Then sew back through the
adjacent hole of the same Quadra-
Tile to change direction **(figure 1)**.

2. Pick up an O-Bead and a
15º, and slide the beads up to the
beadwork. Skip the last 15º picked
up, and sew back through the
O-Bead and the same hole of the
nearest QuadraTile **(figure 2)**.

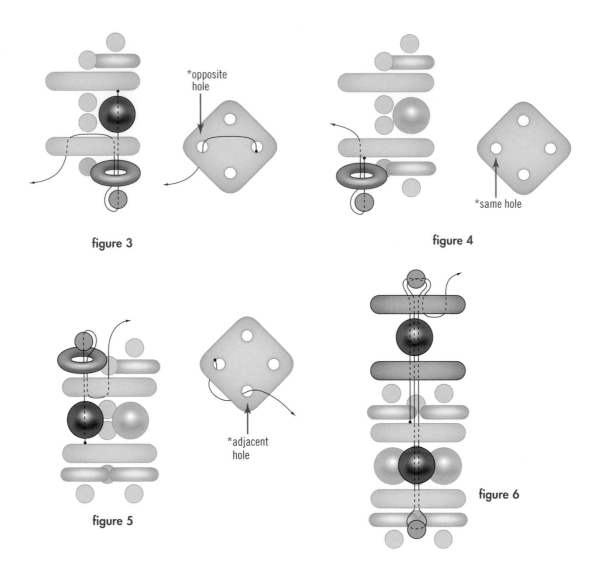

*opposite hole

figure 3

*same hole

figure 4

*adjacent hole

figure 5

figure 6

3. Pick up a 3mm pearl and sew through the corresponding hole of the other QuadraTile. Pick up an O-Bead and a 15º. Slide the beads up to the beadwork. Skip the last 15º picked up. Sew back through the O-Bead and the same hole of the nearest QuadraTile. Sew through the opposite hole of the QuadraTile to change direction **(figure 3)**.

4. Pick up an O-Bead and a 15º, and slide the beads up to the beadwork. Skip the last 15º picked up, and sew back through the O-Bead and the same hole of the nearest QuadraTile **(figure 4)**.

5. Pick up a 3mm, and sew through the corresponding hole of the other QuadraTile. Pick up an O-Bead and a 15º, and slide the beads up to the beadwork. Skip the last 15º picked up, and sew back through the O-Bead and the same hole of the nearest QuadraTile. Sew through the adjacent hole of the same QuadraTile to change direction **(figure 5)**.

SUBSEQUENT UNITS

1. Pick up a new QuadraTile, a 3mm, a QuadraTile, and a 15º, and slide the beads up to the previous unit. Skip the last 15º picked up, and sew back through the same hole

of the nearest QuadraTile. Continue through the next 3mm and the same hole of the next two QuadraTiles. Pick up a 3mm and sew through the open hole of the next QuadraTile in the previous unit. Pick up a 15º, and sew back through the same hole of the nearest QuadraTile. Retrace the thread path to exit the first 15º picked up in this step. Sew back through the same hole of the nearest QuadraTile. Sew back through the adjacent hole of the QuadraTile to change direction **(figure 6)**.

2. Repeat steps 2–5 of "Make the first unit" to complete this unit.

Design Option

You can make a longer version for a necklace or use two colors of QuadraTile beads.

3. Work step 1 of "Subsequent units" to begin each new unit, and then work steps 2–5 of "Make the first unit" to complete each new unit until you reach the desired length.

4. In the last unit, swap out two 15°s for the 3mm opposite the last join. Retrace the thread path several times to reinforce the 15°s. End the working thread and tail (Techniques, p. 13). Add two 15°s to the other end of the bracelet in the same way. Attach a clasp to the two 15°s at each end of the bracelet using jump rings (Techniques).

Ringed Rivoli Pendant

SURROUND A RIVOLI IN A NETWORK OF FOUR-HOLE BEADS, LEAVING PLENTY OF PLACES FOR NETTING EMBELLISHMENTS. THIS LOVELY PIECE WOULD BE AT HOME ON A SIMPLE CHAIN, WIRE, OR LEATHER CORD.

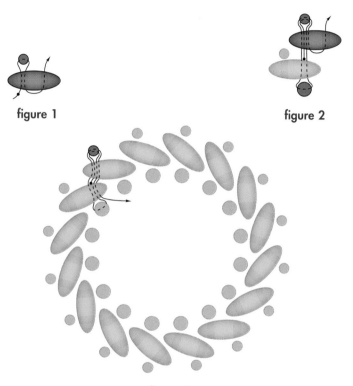

figure 1

figure 2

figure 3

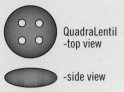

QuadraLentil
-top view

-side view

15º seed bead

11º seed bead

 true 2mm fire-
polished bead

CZECHMATES
QuadraLentil or QuadraTile beads

TECHNIQUES
Netting, p. 13
Adding and Ending Thread, p. 13

SKILL LEVEL
Intermediate ●●●

SUPPLIES
- 14–16mm rivoli
- **16** QuadraLentil beads
- **80** 2mm fire-polished beads
- 2g 11º seed beads
- 2g 15º seed beads (1g each of **2** colors, if desired)
- Fireline, 6- or 8-lb. test
- Beading needle, #12
- Finished neck chain

MAKE THE PENDANT

1. Thread a needle on 2 yd. (1.8m) of Fireline. Pick up a QuadraLentil bead and a 15º seed bead, and center them on the thread. Sew back through the same hole of the QuadraLentil, and then sew through the opposite hole of the same QuadraLentil (**figure 1**).

2. Pick up a new QuadraLentil and a 15º, and sew back through the same hole of the new QuadraLentil and the corresponding hole of the previous QuadraLentil. Pick up an 11º seed bead, the same two holes of the QuadraLentils, and the 15º picked up in this step. Sew back through the same hole of the new QuadraLentil, and then sew through the opposite hole of the new QuadraLentil (**figure 2**).

3. Repeat step 2 until you have 16 QuadraLentils. To make a ring, join the first and last QuadraLentils: Sew up through the corresponding hole of the first QuadraLentil, pick up a 15º, and continue as in step 2 (**figure 3**). Set the working thread aside.

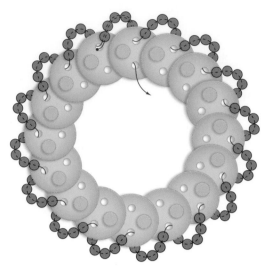

figure 4

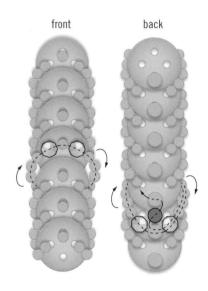

front   back

figure 5

4. Using the tail, sew up through an open hole along one edge. Pick up five 15ºs (switching to another color if desired), and sew up through the open hole of the next QuadraLentil along the same edge. Repeat to complete this edge, and then sew up through the opposite hole of the same QuadraLentil to exit an open hole along the other edge **(figure 4)**. Repeat this step to complete the embellishment along the other edge.

5. Sew through the nearest five 15ºs, pick up a 2mm fire-polished bead, and then sew through the next 15º, pick up a 2mm, and then sew through the next five 15ºs. Sew through the first 2mm and following 11º. Pick up an 11º, and then sew through the next 11º along the inside edge of the beadwork **(figure 5)**. Continue adding 2mms in the same manner until you finish the embellishment. Exit an 11º added in this step along the inner ring.

6. Pick up two 15ºs, an 11º, and two 15ºs. Skip three 11ºs and sew through the next 11º in the inner ring **(figure 6, a–b)**. Repeat around the ring, and then step up through the first two 15ºs and 11º picked up in this round **(b–c)**.

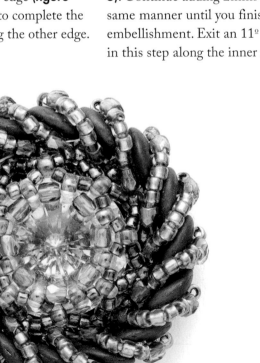

PENDANT FRONT

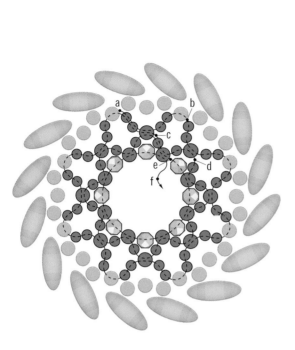

figure 6

7. Pick up a 15º, an 11º, and a 15º. Sew through the center 11º in the next stitch of the previous round (c–d). Repeat around the ring and then step up through the first 15º and 11º picked up in this round (d–e).

8. Pick up a 2mm and sew through the center 11º in the next stitch of the previous round. Repeat around the ring (e–f), and then retrace the thread pattern of the new ring of 2mms.

9. Repeat steps 6–8 with the other thread on the back of the pendant, but before finishing step 8, slip the rivoli into the netted beadwork. Choose either size seed bead and make a loop of nine 11ºs or 11 15ºs on one side (exit an 11º, skip an 11º, and sew into the next 11º) and end the threads (Techniques, p. 13).

10. Slide the pendant on a finished neck chain.

PENDANT SIDE

Triangle Tulips Bracelet

WEAVE LITTLE FLORAL COMPONENTS IN A ZIGZAG PATH AND EDGE IT WITH SPARKLING CRYSTALS. YOU COULD ALSO STITCH A LONGER LENGTH TO MAKE AN EYE-CATCHING CHOKER.

figure 1

MAKE THE BRACELET

1. Lay out three Triangle beads so the holes are on the bottom, closest to you, and the point without holes is pointing away from you **(figure 1)**. Thread a needle and attach a stop bead to the end of 2 yd. (1.8m) of Fireline, leaving a 10-in. (25cm) tail.

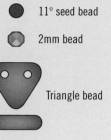

- 11º seed bead
- 2mm bead
- Triangle bead
- 3mm bicone crystal
- 15º seed bead

CZECHMATES
Triangle or Bar beads

TECHNIQUES
- Modified Right-Angle Weave, p. 17
- Adding and Ending Thread, p. 13
- Stop Beads, p. 13

SKILL LEVEL
Intermediate ● ● ●

SUPPLIES
- **36–42** Triangle beads
- **76–86** true 2mm fire-polished or rondelle crystals
- **22–26** 3mm bicone crystals
- 4g 11º seed beads
- 3g 15º seed beads
- Fireline, 6- or 8-lb. test
- Beading needles, #12
- Clasp
- **2** jump rings
- **2** pairs of chainnose pliers

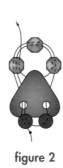

figure 2

figure 3

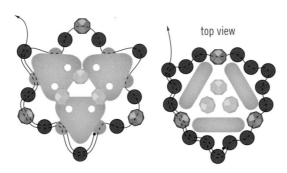

top view

figure 4

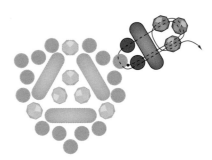

figure 5

2. Pick up an 11º and sew through the left hole of a Triangle from the top down. Pick up three 2mms, and sew through the open hole of the Triangle just picked up in the opposite direction. Pick up an 11º, and sew through the first 11º picked up in this step and the corresponding hole of the Triangle. Retrace the thread path of the three 2mms to pull them into the ring, exiting the first 2mm picked up **(figure 2)**.

3. Sew through the left hole of a new Triangle from the top down. Pick up two 11ºs, sew through the open hole of the same Triangle in the opposite direction, and then sew through the next 2mm in the ring. Repeat this step once more, and then exit the corresponding hole of the next Triangle and the following 11º **(figure 3)**.

4. Flip the beadwork over. Pick up an 11º, a 2mm, and an 11º, and sew through the next 11º. Repeat. Pick up an 11º, and sew through the next 11º. Repeat this step twice. Then sew through the beadwork to exit the center 11º adjacent to the next Triangle in the ring **(figure 4)**.

5. Pick up an 11º and sew through the right hole of a new Triangle from top down. Pick up three 2mms, and sew through the open hole of the Triangle just picked up in the opposite direction. Pick up an 11º, sew through the center 11º your thread just exited, the following 11º, and the corresponding hole of the Triangle. Sew through the three 2mms to pull them into the ring, and exit the first 2mm picked up **(figure 5)**.

6. Sew through the right hole of a new Triangle from the top down. Pick up two 11ºs, sew through the open hole of the same Triangle in the opposite direction, and then sew through the next 2mm in the ring. Repeat this step once more, and then sew through the corresponding hole of the next Triangle and the following 11º. Skip the center 11º joining the two tulip components, and sew through the following 11º **(figure 6)**.

7. Pick up an 11º, a 2mm, and an 11º, and sew through the next 11º. Pick up an 11º, and sew through the next 11º. Repeat this step, and then pick up an 11º, a 2mm, and an 11º, and sew through the next 11º. Sew through the next seven beads to exit the center 11º adjacent to the next Triangle in the ring **(figure 7)**.

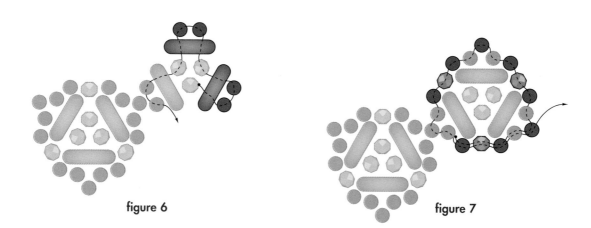

figure 6

figure 7

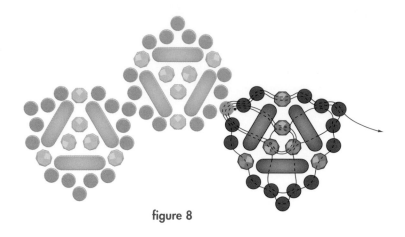

figure 8

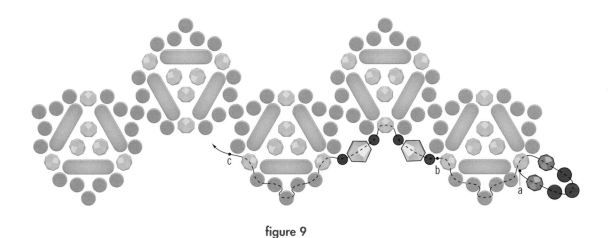

figure 9

8. Work as in steps 5–7 to make the next tulip component **(figure 8)**, but pick up the Triangle beads through the left hole first. (A good rule of thumb is to lay out the beadwork with the thread exiting the top edge, and look at the beadwork from the top down. See which side of the center 11º your thread is exiting. If it is exiting to the left, sew through the left hole of the Triangles first, from top down, and if it exits to the right of the center 11º, pick up the right hole of the Triangles first, from top down. The important thing is that all the Triangles are pointing the same way, and the beadwork zigzags slightly.) Repeat until you have the desired number of components.

9. Exit an end 2mm. Pick up a 2mm, three 11ºs, and a 2mm. Sew through the 2mm your thread exited at the start of this step to make a loop for the clasp, and reinforce a few times. Sew through the beadwork to exit a 2mm along either edge of the bracelet **(figure 9, a–b)**.

10. Pick up a 15º, a 3mm bicone, and a 15º. Sew through the next 2mm along this edge. Repeat once. Sew through the next five 11ºs and following 2mm **(b–c)**.

11. Repeat step 10 to complete the 3mm embellishments along this edge, and then exit the end 2mm. Repeat step 9 to add a loop for the clasp on this end. Continue the 3mm embellishment along the other edge, and then end the working thread and tail.

12. Attach the clasp with jump rings (Techniques, p. 13).

Color Option

Choose a high-contrast color palette that allows the Triangle beads in the design to pop.

Design Option

Make shorter strips of beadwork to create a smashing pair of earrings. Only work step 9 on one end of the beadwork to create a loop to attach an earring finding. A single component makes a nice little earring as well.

Triple-Threat Cuff

MAKE A STATEMENT WITH THIS FLORAL MOTIF IN A WIDE STITCHED CUFF. AFTER GETTING THE TECHNIQUE DOWN, TRY USING TRIANGLE BEADS TO MAKE THE DESIGN REALLY STAND OUT.

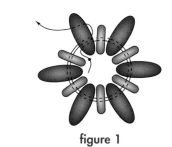

figure 1

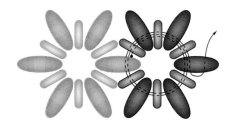

figure 2

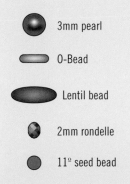

3mm pearl

O-Bead

Lentil bead

2mm rondelle

11º seed bead

CZECHMATES
Lentil or Triangle beads

TECHNIQUES
- Adding and Ending Thread, p. 13
- Right-Angle Weave, p. 17

SKILL LEVEL
Intermediate ● ● ●

SUPPLIES
- **150** Lentil beads
- **420** O-Beads
- **90** 3mm round beads or pearls
- **135** 2mm rondelle crystals
- 4g 11º seed beads
- Fireline, 6- or 8-lb. test
- Beading needle, #12

MAKE THE CUFF

1. Thread a needle on 4 yd. (3.7m) of Fireline. Pick up a repeating pattern of a Lentil bead and a O-Bead six times, and center them on the thread. Scw through all the beads again to form a ring and then sew through the same hole of the next Lentil to exit next to the tail. Tie the working thread and tail together. Sew through the other hole of the same Lentil to change direction **(figure 1)**.

2. Pick up a repeating pattern of an O-Bead and a Lentil five times and then pick up an O-Bead. Sew through the same hole of the Lentil your thread exited at the start of this step. Retrace the thread path of the new ring, and then sew through the ring to exit the Lentil opposite the shared Lentil. Sew through the other hole of the same Lentil to change direction **(figure 2)**. Repeat this step until you reach the desired length.

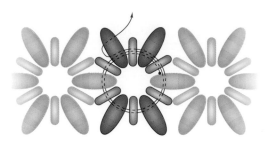

figure 3

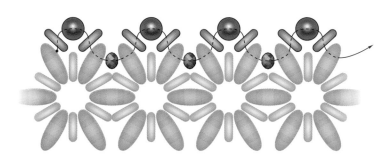

figure 4

3. Pick up a repeating pattern of an O-Bead and a Lentil twice, and then pick up an O-Bead. Sew through the open hole of the Lentil in the first unit opposite the previous shared Lentil. Pick up a repeating pattern of an O-Bead and a Lentil twice, and then pick up an O-Bead. Sew through the open hole of the Lentil in the last unit opposite the previous shared Lentil. Retrace the thread path of the new ring, and then exit the second Lentil picked up in this step. Sew through the other hole of the same Lentil to change direction **(figure 3)**.

4. Pick up an O-Bead, a 3mm round bead, and an O-Bead. Sew through the open hole of the next Lentil along this edge. Pick up a 2mm rondelle, and sew through the open hole of the next Lentil along

this edge. Repeat **(figure 4)** this step to complete the round, and exit a 3mm picked up in this step.

5. Pick up an 11º, an O-Bead, a Lentil, an O-Bead, and an 11º. Sew through the same 3mm your thread exited at the start of this step, and the same holes of the first four beads picked up **(figure 5, a–b)**.

6. Pick up an 11º, a 3mm, an 11º, an O-Bead, a Lentil, an O-Bead, and an 11º. Sew back through the next 3mm in the previous round, and then pick up an 11º. Sew through the O-Bead, the same hole of the Lentil, and the O-Bead **(b–c)**. Repeat this step to complete the round, and exit a Lentil. Sew through the other hole of the same Lentil to change direction **(c–d)**.

7. Pick up an O-Bead, a 2mm, an O-Bead, a 2mm, and an O-Bead. Sew through the open hole of the next Lentil along this edge. Repeat **(figure 6)** to complete the round. Retrace the thread path around the edge, and then end the thread (Techniques, p. 13).

8. Repeat steps 4–7 along the other edge using the tail.

Tip
To tackle a slightly tougher project, use Triangle beads. When you pick them up, be sure to keep all the points facing the same direction.

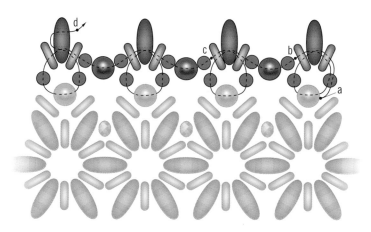

figure 5

figure 6

Design Option

Use Triangle beads for a cuff with even more dimension and texture.

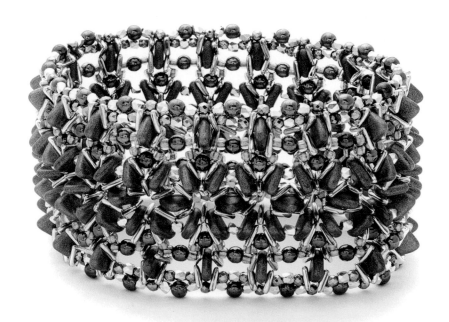

Twin Tracks Bracelet

LAY DOWN TRACKS TO STYLE WITH THIS QUICK
CROSSWEAVE TECHNIQUE INCORPORATING LOVELY
LENTIL BEADS AND SPARKLING CRYSTALS. THIS EASY-TO-
WEAR BRACELET COMES TOGETHER IN A SNAP.

 3mm bicone

 Lentil bead

 15º seed bead

CZECHMATES
Lentil or Bar beads

TECHNIQUES
- Opening and Closing Jump Rings, p. 13
- Adding and Ending Thread, p. 13
- Crossweave Technique, p. 16

SKILL LEVEL
Beginner ⬤ ◯ ◯

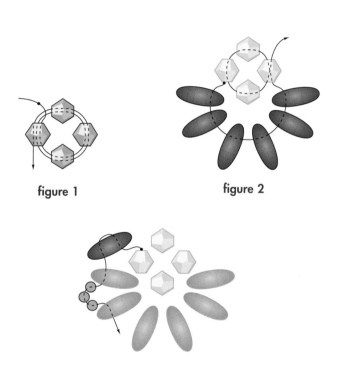

figure 1

figure 2

figure 3

SUPPLIES
- **120** Lentil beads
- **140** 3mm bicone crystals
- **6** 15º seed beads
- Fireline, 6- or 8-lb. test
- **2** beading needles, #12
- 2-part clasp
- **2** 4–6mm jump rings
- **2** pairs of chainnose pliers

MAKE THE BRACELET

1. Thread a needle on each end of 3 yd. (2.7m) of Fireline. On one needle, center four 3mm bicone crystals and sew through all the 3mms again so one thread exits each end of the first 3mm picked up **(figure 1)**.

2. With the same needle, pick up six Lentil beads. Sew through the opposite 3mm from where you exited at the start of this step **(figure 2)**.

3. With the other needle, pick up a Lentil and snug it up to the beadwork. Sew through the remaining hole of the same Lentil and the open hole of the next Lentil. Pick up three 15º seed beads and sew through the remaining hole of the next Lentil **(figure 3)**.

4. With the same needle, pick up a 3mm, and sew through the remaining hole of the next Lentil. Repeat this step twice and then pick up four 3mms. Sew through the first 3mm again, and then sew through the remaining hole of the next Lentil **(figure 4)**.

5. With the same needle, pick up five Lentils, skip the next 3mm, and then sew through the following 3mm **(figure 5)**. Retrace the thread path of the four 3mms to secure the thread and reinforce the 3mms.

6. With the other needle, sew through the remaining hole of the next Lentil. Pick up a 3mm, and sew through the remaining hole of the next Lentil. Repeat the last stitch to add 3mms between the next two Lentils. Pick up four 3mms and sew through the first 3mm just picked up and the remaining hole of the next Lentil **(figure 6)**.

7. With the same needle, pick up five Lentils, skip the next 3mm, and sew through the following 3mm **(figure 7)**. Retrace the thread path of the four 3mms to secure the thread and reinforce the 3mms.

8. With the other needle, sew through the remaining hole of the next Lentil. Pick up a 3mm, and sew through the remaining hole of the next Lentil. Repeat the last stitch to add two more 3mms between the next two Lentils. Pick up four 3mms, and sew through the first 3mm just picked up and the remaining hole of the next Lentil **(figure 8)**.

9. Repeat steps 5–8 until you have reached the desired length, ending on step 7.

10. With the same needle, pick up one Lentil. Snug the bead up to the beadwork and then sew through the remaining hole of the same Lentil. Sew through the open hole of the next Lentil. Pick up three 15⁰s and sew through the remaining hole of the next Lentil. Pick up a 3mm, and sew through the remaining hole of the next Lentil. Repeat the last stitch two more times, and end the thread (Techniques, p. 13) **(figure 9)**.

11. Retrace the thread path with the other needle and end the remaining thread.

12. Attach the clasp to each space between the two Lentils with the three 15⁰s on each end using jump rings (Techniques).

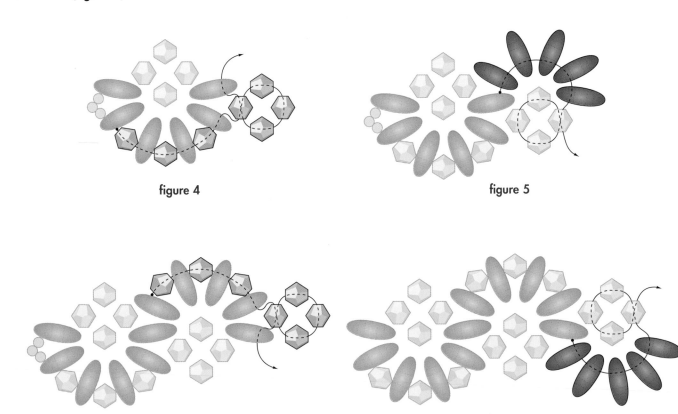

figure 4

figure 5

figure 6

figure 7

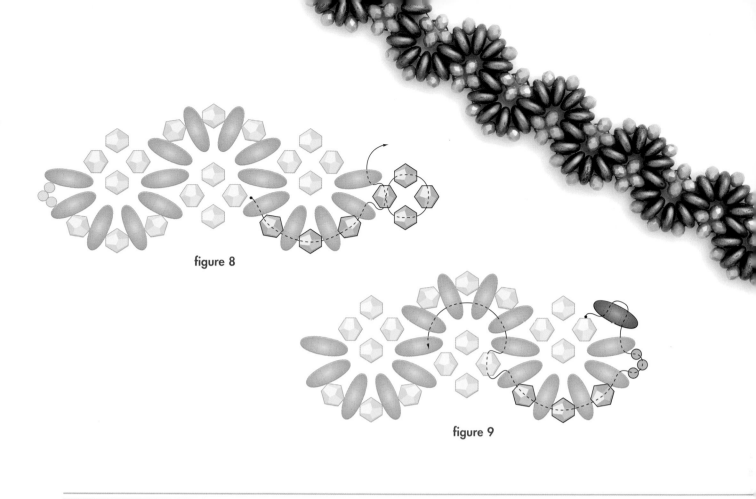

figure 8

figure 9

Design Option

Use a combination of matte glass pearls and bicone crystals instead of fire-polished beads for a more toned-down look.

Water Lily Pendant

CREATE A GORGEOUS FLOWER PENDANT USING SIMPLE TECHNIQUES AND A DISTINCTIVE BEAD. STRING YOUR FINISHED PIECE ON A CORD OF YOUR CHOICE FOR INSTANT, BEAUTIFUL STYLE.

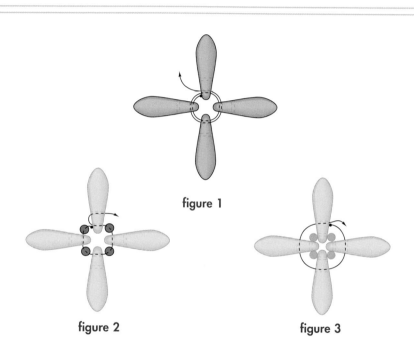

figure 1

figure 2

figure 3

●   11° seed bead

Dagger bead
— top hole
— bottom hole

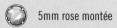
5mm rose montée

CZECHMATES
Dagger beads

TECHNIQUES
- Adding and Ending Thread, p. 13
- Modified Right-Angle Weave, p. 17

SKILL LEVEL
Beginner ●○○

MAKE THE PENDANT

1. Thread a needle and attach a stop bead to 1½ yd. (1.4m) of Fireline, leaving an 18-in. (46cm) tail.

2. Sew through the bottom hole of four Dagger beads. Sew through the same hole of all the Daggers again, and exit the same hole of the first Dagger picked up **(figure 1)**.

3. Pick up an 11°, and sew through the same hole of the next Dagger. Repeat this step three times, and then sew through the other hole of the same Dagger your thread is exiting to change direction **(figure 2)**.

4. Sew through the top hole of the next Dagger. Repeat this step three times **(figure 3)**.

SUPPLIES
- **16** Dagger beads
- 5mm rose montée
- 2–3g 11° seed beads
- Fireline, 6- or 8-lb. test
- Beading needles, #12
- 6mm jump ring
- **2** pairs of chainnose pliers
- Finished neck chain

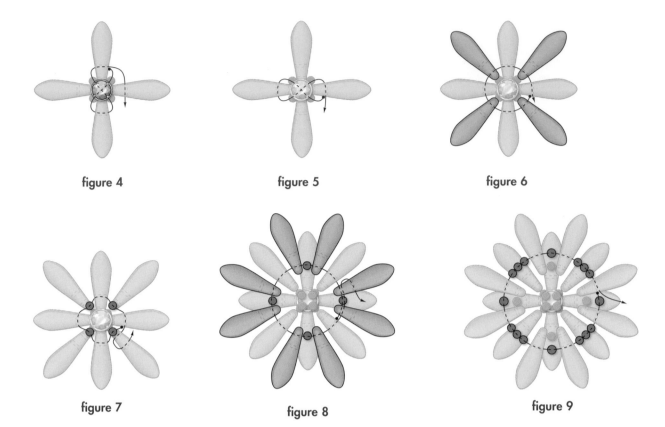

figure 4

figure 5

figure 6

figure 7

figure 8

figure 9

5. Sew through one hole of a rose montée, and sew through the top hole of the Dagger opposite the Dagger your thread exited at the start of this step. Sew through the other hole of the rose montée, and through the top hole of the Dagger your thread exited at the start of this step **(figure 4)**. Sew through the top hole of the next Dagger. Retrace the thread path through the rose montée and the opposite Dagger to secure the rose montée, and exit the top hole of a Dagger **(figure 5)**.

6. Sew through the bottom hole of a new Dagger, and sew through the top hole of the next Dagger in the initial round. Repeat this step three times, retrace the thread path, and exit the top hole of a Dagger in the initial round **(figure 6)**.

7. Pick up an 11º seed bead, and sew through the top hole of the next Dagger in the initial round, positioning the 11º to sit at the edge of the rose montée. Repeat this step three times, and exit the bottom hole of a Dagger in the outer round. Sew through the open hole of the same Dagger to change direction **(figure 7)**.

8. Pick up the bottom hole of a new Dagger, an 11º, and the bottom hole of another new Dagger. Sew through the top hole of the next Dagger in the previous round. Repeat this step three times, retrace the thread path, and exit a bottom hole of the second Dagger in a set of two Daggers picked up in the new outer round. Sew through the open hole of the same Dagger to change direction. Your thread should be

exiting above an 11º in the outer round **(figure 8)**.

9. Pick up an 11º, and sew through the top hole of the next Dagger in the outer round. Pick up three 11ºs, and sew through the top hole of the next Dagger in the outer round. The three 11ºs will sit along the outer edge of a Dagger in the previous round. Repeat this step three times **(figure 9)**, retrace the thread path, and end the working thread (Techniques, p. 13).

10. Remove the stop bead, and make sure the tail is exiting an 11º in the initial round.

11. Pick up five 11ºs, and sew back through the center 11º in the outer ring, directly above the 11º your tail is exiting. Pick up five 11ºs, and sew through the same 11º your thread

figure 10

figure 11

PENDANT BACK

exited at the start of this step, the bottom hole of the next Dagger, and the following 11º in the initial ring. Repeat this step three times, retrace the thread path, and exit a center 11º in the outer round (**figure 10**).

12. Pick up eleven 11ºs, and sew through the 11º your thread exited at the start of this step (**figure 11**). Retrace the thread path several times, and end the thread (Techniques). (As an alternate, you can repeat this step on the center 11º in the next set of three 11ºs to create two points for attaching a chain or other beadwork.)

13. Open a jump ring and attach the pendant loop (Techniques). Slide the pendant on a neck chain.

Color Options

Wrap Bracelet

MAKE THIS SLINKY WRAP BRACELET, WHICH COULD ALSO WORK NICELY AS A NECKLACE. LENTIL OR BAR BEADS NESTLE RIGHT INTO PLACE, RESULTING IN AN EASY-TO-STITCH PIECE OF JEWELRY.

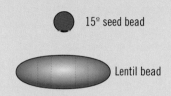

15º seed bead

Lentil bead

CZECHMATES
Lentil or Bar beads

TECHNIQUES
- Adding and Ending Thread, p. 13
- Opening and Closing Jump Rings, p. 13
- Modified Herringbone, p. 14

SKILL LEVEL
Beginner ●○○

MATERIALS
- **160–175** Lentil beads
- 4g 15º seed beads
- 2-part clasp
- **2** 6mm jump rings (optional)
- Fireline, 8-lb. test
- Beading needles, #12
- **2** pairs of chainnose pliers

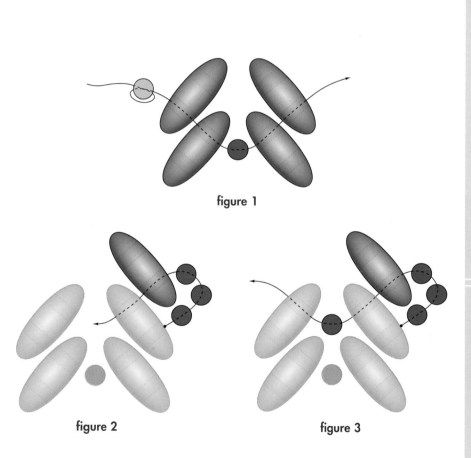

figure 1

figure 2

figure 3

MAKE THE BRACELET

1. Thread a needle and attach a stop bead on 2–3yd. (1.8–2.7m) of Fireline, leaving a 12-in. (30cm) tail.

2. Pick up two Lentil beads, a 15º seed bead, and two Lentils **(figure 1)**.

3. Pick up three 15ºs and a Lentil. Sew through the open hole of the last Lentil picked up in the previous step **(figure 2)**.

4. Pick up a 15º, and sew through the open hole of the first Lentil picked up in step 1 **(figure 3)**.

5. Pick up a Lentil and three 15ºs. Sew back through the other hole of the Lentil your thread exited at the start of this step, the corresponding hole of the next Lentil, the center 15º, and the corresponding holes of the next two Lentils along the other edge of the bracelet **(figure 4, a–b)**.

6. Without picking up any beads, retrace the thread path through the next three 15ºs, back through the corresponding holes of the next two Lentils, the center 15º, and the corresponding two holes of the next two Lentils along the other edge of the bracelet **(b–c)**.

7. Pick up three 15ºs and a Lentil. Sew through the open hole of the Lentil your thread exited at the start of this step. Pick up a 15º, and sew through the open hole of the Lentil along the other edge of the bracelet.

8. Repeat steps 5–7 until you reach the desired length, ending on step 6.

9. Using the working thread, pick up three 15ºs, and sew through the open hole of the end Lentil. Pick up a 15º, and sew through the open hole of the Lentil along the other edge of the bracelet. Pick up three 15ºs, and sew through the other hole of the same Lentil, the corresponding hole of the following Lentil, the center 15º, and the corresponding holes of the two Lentils along the other edge **(figure 5, a–b)**. Retrace the thread path several times, and then end the thread (Techniques, p. 13). (You can also pick up half of a two-part clasp in place of the center 15º.)

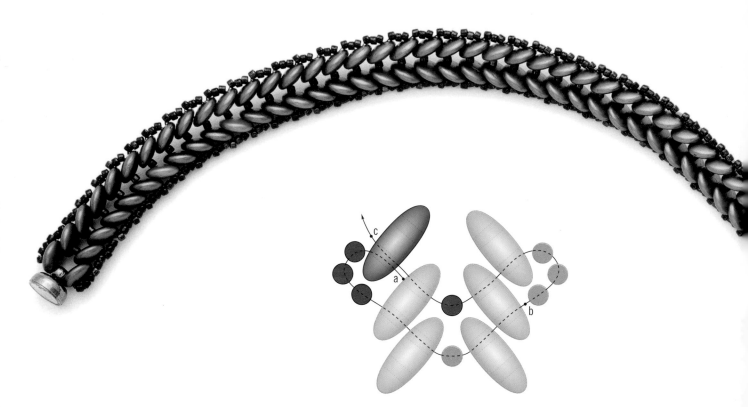

figure 4

10. Remove the stop bead. Using the tail, pick up three 15°s, and sew through the open hole of the end Lentil. Pick up three 15°s (if desired, pick up half the clasp in place of the middle 15°), and sew through the open hole of the end Lentil along the other edge. Pick up three 15°s, and sew back through the corresponding holes of the last two Lentils on this edge, the center 15°, and the corresponding holes of the two Lentils on the other edge (c–d). Retrace the thread path, and end the tail.

11. Attach a clasp half to each end with jump rings (optional) (Techniques).

Design Option

You can use Bar beads in place of Lentil beads. You can also make a shorter bracelet or a choker-style necklace using the same technique.

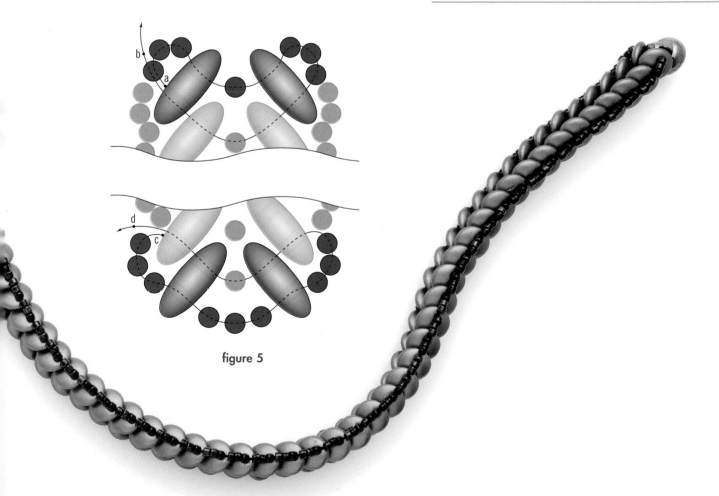

figure 5

Bricks and Honeycombs Bracelet

WEAVE A GEOMETRIC GEM USING BRICK BEADS, HONEYCOMB BEADS, AND PEARLS. TRY MIXING UP YOUR COLOR PALETTE BY CHOOSING CONTRASTING HUES FOR EVEN MORE INTEREST.

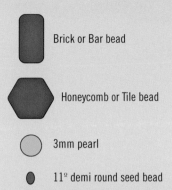

Brick or Bar bead

Honeycomb or Tile bead

3mm pearl

11º demi round seed bead

CZECHMATES
Brick or Bar beads (Tile beads optional)

TECHNIQUES
Right-Angle Weave, p. 17

SKILL LEVEL
Beginner ⬤ ◯ ◯

MATERIALS
- **58** 3mm pearls
- **9** faceted or flat Honeycomb beads or Tile beads
- **36** Brick or Bar beads
- 3g 11º demi round seed beads
- Fireline, 6- or 8-lb. test
- Beading needles, #12
- **2–4** 6mm jump rings
- Two-part clasp
- **2** pairs of chainnose pliers

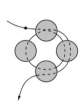

figure 1

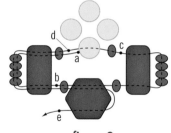

figure 2

MAKE THE BRACELET

1. Thread a needle on 3 yd. (2.7m) of Fireline, and pick up four 3mm pearls. Sew through all the pearls to form a ring, and then sew through the first three pearls again to exit opposite the tail, leaving a 24-in. (61cm) tail **(figure 1)**.

2. Pick up an 11º demi round seed bead and a Brick bead. Pick up four 11ºs, and sew back through the open hole of the same Brick **(figure 2, a–b)**.

3. Pick up an 11º, a Honeycomb bead, an 11º, a Brick, and four 11ºs. Sew back through the open hole of the same Brick **(b–c)**.

4. Pick up an 11º, and sew through the pearl your thread exited at the start of step 2 **(c–d)**.

5. Sew through the same holes of the first nine beads picked up, and then sew through the open hole of the Honeycomb **(d–e)**.

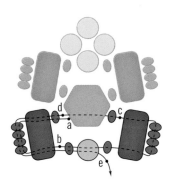

figure 3

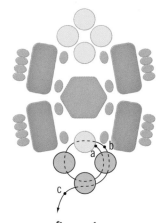

figure 4

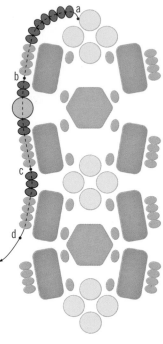

figure 5

6. Pick up an 11º and a Brick. Pick up four 11ºs, and sew back through the open hole of the same Brick (**figure 3, a–b**).

7. Pick up an 11º, a pearl, an 11º, a Brick, and four 11ºs. Sew back through the open hole of the same Brick (**b–c**).

8. Pick up an 11º, and sew through the Honeycomb your thread exited at the start of this step (**c–d**).

9. Sew through the same holes of the first nine beads picked up (**d–e**).

10. Pick up three pearls, and sew through the pearl your thread exited at the start of this step to form a ring (**figure 4, a–b**). Sew through the next two pearls (**b–c**).

11. Repeat steps 2–10 until you reach the desired length. End the working thread.

12. Using the tail, pick up seven 11ºs, and sew through the next four 11ºs along this edge (**figure 5, a–b**).

13. Pick up two 11ºs, a pearl, and two 11ºs. Sew through the next four 11ºs along this edge (**b–c**).

14. Pick up three 11ºs, and sew through the next four 11ºs (**c–d**).

15. Repeat steps 13 and 14 until you reach the other end. Work as in step 12 on each side of the end pearl unit, and then continue steps 13 and 14 along the other edge. Retrace the outer edge if desired, and end the tail.

16. Open the jump rings, and attach half the clasp to an end pearl unit with one or two rings (Techniques, p. 13). Repeat on the other end of the bracelet.

Anna's Gallery

Anna's Gallery

FIGURE-8 BRACELET

TRIANGLE BRACELET

CRISS-CROSS BRACELET

LACY CUFF

BUBBLE BANGLE

PEBBLE PATH
BRACELET

CRESCENT RING

TILE BRACELET

Anna's Gallery

CONNECTED RINGS BRACELET

LACY EDGE CUFF

DOMED BEADED BEADS

LAVENDER BRACELET

WINDING BRICK NECKLACE

SEED BEAD
SPLENDOR BRACELET

GLOWING
RING

SQUARE LINK
BRACELET

109

Acknowledgments

I would like to thank my family for their patience and support.

Thanks also to the team at Kalmbach Publishing Co.: Lisa Schroeder, book artist, Dana Meredith, tech editor, Bill Zuback, photographer, Erica Barse, editor, and Dianne Wheeler, editor-in-chief.

And as always, I thank my readers and fans, whose interest in my work keeps me creating.

About the Author

Anna Elizabeth Draeger is a well-known jewelry designer, former associate editor for *Bead&Button magazine,* and the author of *Crystal Brilliance, Creative Designs Using Shaped Beads, More Great Designs for Shaped Beads, Crystal Play,* and *Classic Stitching.* Anna was an ambassador for the Create Your Style with Swarovski Elements program, a handpicked worldwide network of artists who are known for their design expertise and passion for teaching. Reach Anna at beadbiz@mac.com, or shop for jewelry and kits at: annaelizabethdraeger.etsy.com.

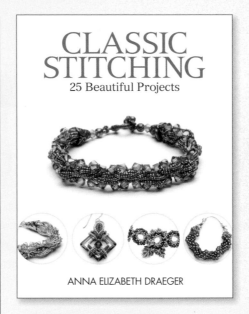
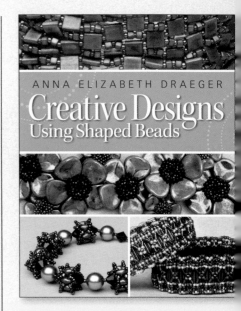